# THE CIVIL LAW TRADITION

# THE CIVIL LAW
# TRADITION

An Introduction to the Legal Systems of Western Europe
and Latin America

JOHN HENRY MERRYMAN

STANFORD UNIVERSITY PRESS

STANFORD, CALIFORNIA

1969

Stanford University Press
Stanford, California
© 1969 by the Board of Trustees of the
Leland Stanford Junior University
Printed in the United States of America
L.C. 70-83118
Cloth SBN 8047–0694–8
Paper SBN 8047–0695–6

*For Nancy, Len, Sam, and Bruce,*
*in celebration of April 1, 1953,*
*and other great days.*

# PREFACE

THIS BOOK is written for amateurs, not professionals. It speaks to the general reader who wants to know what it is that binds together the legal systems of Western Europe and Latin America, and that distinguishes them from the legal systems of the Anglo-American world; to the nonlawyer who wishes to know something about the legal side of European and Latin American culture; to the student seeking collateral reading for a course in history, politics, sociology, philosophy, international relations, area studies, or law. This book may also have some use among lawyers who have not studied foreign and comparative law and wish, for practical or other reasons, to begin to remedy this deficiency. It can provide background reading for persons with public or private business in Europe or Latin America (or other civil law nations). My professional colleagues in foreign and comparative law, however, are likely to find the work too elementary and too general to engage their interest.

Although I have tried to make it clear in the text that this book does not attempt to describe any specific national legal system, a special word should be said here about the peculiar problem posed by France and Germany. Each of these nations has made a major contribution to the civil law tradition, and each still occupies a position of intellectual leadership in the civil law world. At the same time, neither is a "typical" civil law system. Indeed, both are in a sense the least typical of all. The French revolutionary ideology and the French style of codification had only a limited impact on German law. German legal science has never really caught on in France. Elsewhere in the civil law world, however, there has been a strong tendency to receive and fuse both influences. This is particularly true in Mediterranean Europe and Latin America, but it also applies to some extent to most other parts of the civil law world. A French or German reader

may find much in this book that is not representative of his legal system. The reason is that his system is atypical. The civil law world includes a great number of national legal systems in Europe, Latin America, Asia, Africa, and the Middle East. This book is about the legal tradition they share, not about French or German law.

Something should also be said about perspective. I do not mean to suggest that all lawyers in civil law nations accept and believe in those aspects of their tradition that will appear to the reader to be excessive or deficient. On the contrary, I have tried to indicate throughout (and to hammer the point home once again in Chapter XIX, which I beg the reader not to skip) that I am describing "prevailing" attitudes. There is the common run of lawyers, and there is the sophisticated, critical jurist at the growing point of legal thought. Sophisticated jurists always constitute the smaller and less representative group, but even in the most backward nation one can expect to find a few lawyers who will say: "I don't think that way at all." In a more advanced civil law nation like France or Germany, the proportion of enlightened and liberated lawyers and the extent to which the legal order has freed itself of the defects of the tradition will be greater. That is another indication of the atypicality of France and Germany. This book, however, is about the way the common run of lawyers in the civil law world generally think, even though the avant-garde of legal thought tells them they are wrong.

Dean Bayless A. Manning of the Stanford School of Law persuaded me that there was a need for this book, and encouraged me to write it. Three outstanding comparative lawyers—Professors Mauro Cappelletti of the University of Florence, F. H. Lawson, formerly of Oxford University, and Konrad Zweigert, of the Max Planck Institute in Hamburg—kindly read the manuscript and suggested a number of changes that improved it. One of my colleagues at Stanford, Dr. George Torzsay-Biber, was particularly helpful on a number of questions concerning Roman civil law. Generations of imaginative and industrious scholars have produced a rich literature on foreign and comparative law, from which most of the ideas contained in this book were drawn. Dr. Hein Kötz, Research Associate at the Max Planck

Institute, and Gernot Reiners, a Teaching Fellow at the Stanford School of Law, 1967–68, assisted me in a variety of ways, and in particular gave me authoritative information on German law. Mrs. Lois St. John Rigg prepared the manuscript for publication with skill, patience, and good humor. To all, my thanks.

J.H.M.

*Stanford*
*1969*

# CONTENTS

# THE CIVIL LAW TRADITION

# I

## THREE LEGAL TRADITIONS

THERE ARE three major legal traditions in the contemporary world: civil law, common law, and socialist law. This book is about the oldest, most widely distributed, and most influential of them: the civil law tradition.

The reader will observe that the term used is "legal tradition," not "legal system." The purpose is to distinguish between two quite different ideas. A legal system, as that term is here used, is an operating set of legal institutions, procedures, and rules. In this sense there are one federal and fifty state legal systems in the United States, separate legal systems in each of the other nations, and still other distinct legal systems in such organizations as the European Economic Community and the United Nations. In a world organized into sovereign states and organizations of states, there are as many legal systems as there are such states and organizations.

National legal systems are frequently classified into groups or families. Thus the legal systems of England, New Zealand, California, and New York are called "common law" systems, and there are good reasons to group them together in this way. But it is inaccurate to suggest that they have identical legal institutions, processes, and rules. On the contrary, there is great diversity among them, not only in their substantive rules of law, but also in their institutions and processes.

Similarly, France, Germany, Italy, and Switzerland have their own legal systems, as do Argentina, Brazil, and Chile. It is true that they are all frequently spoken of as "civil law" nations, and we will try in this book to explain why it makes sense to group them together in this way. But it is important to recognize that there are great differences between the operating legal systems in these countries. They have quite different legal rules, legal procedures, and legal institutions. Even in Eastern Europe, despite the strong forces tending to produce uniformity within the Soviet sphere of influence, a similar, if less pro-

nounced, diversity exists. Although these nations are commonly lumped together as "socialist law" nations, there is a great deal of variation among them, even in fundamental matters. For example, all land in the Soviet Union is owned by the state, but most other socialist nations permit some private ownership of land, even of productive agrarian land. Such differences in legal systems are reflections of the fact that for several centuries the world has been divided up into individual states, under intellectual conditions that have emphasized the importance of state sovereignty and encouraged a nationalistic emphasis on national characteristics and traditions. In this sense, there is no such thing as *the* civil law system, *the* common law system, or *the* socialist law system. Rather, there are many different legal systems within each of these three groups or families of legal systems. But the fact that different legal systems are grouped together under such a rubric as "civil law," for example, indicates that they have something in common, something that distinguishes them from legal systems classified as "common law" or "socialist law." It is this uniquely shared something that is here spoken of as a legal tradition, and that makes it possible to speak of the French and German (and many other) legal systems as civil law systems.

A legal tradition, as the term implies, is not a set of rules of law about contracts, corporations, and crimes, although such rules will almost always be in some sense a reflection of that tradition. Rather it is a set of deeply rooted, historically conditioned attitudes about the nature of law, about the role of law in the society and the polity, about the proper organization and operation of a legal system, and about the way law is or should be made, applied, studied, perfected, and taught. The legal tradition relates the legal system to the culture of which it is a partial expression. It puts the legal system into cultural perspective.

Of the great variety of living legal traditions, the three mentioned above are of particular interest because they are in force in powerful, technologically advanced nations and because they have been exported, with greater or less effect, to other parts of the world. Of the three, the civil law tradition is both the oldest and the most widely distributed. The traditional date of its origin is 450 B.C., the supposed

date of publication of the XII Tables in Rome. It is today the dominant legal tradition in most of Western Europe, all of Central and South America, many parts of Asia and Africa, and even a few enclaves in the common law world (Louisiana, Quebec, and Puerto Rico). It was, until recently, the dominant legal tradition in most of the countries of Eastern Europe (including the Soviet Union), which have since become socialist law countries; hence an understanding of the civil law tradition is essential to an understanding of socialist law. The civil law was the legal tradition familiar to the Western European scholar-politicians who were the fathers of international law. The basic charters and the continuing legal development and operation of the European Communities are the work of people trained in the civil law tradition. It is difficult to overstate the influence of the civil law tradition on the law of specific nations, the law of international organizations, and international law.

We in the common law world are not accustomed to thinking in these terms. Hence it bears repeating that the civil law tradition is older, more widely distributed, and more influential than the common law tradition. In these senses, at least, it is more important. It should be added that many people believe the civil law to be culturally superior to the common law, which seems to them to be relatively crude and unorganized. The question of superiority is really beside the point. Sophisticated comparative lawyers within both traditions long ago abandoned discussions of relative superiority or inferiority. But it is to the point that many people think that their legal system is superior to ours. That attitude itself has become part of the civil law tradition.

Hence a lawyer from a relatively undeveloped nation in Central America may be convinced that his legal system is measurably superior to that of the United States or Canada. Unless he is a very sophisticated student of comparative law, he may be inclined to patronize a common lawyer. He will recognize our more advanced economic development, and he may envy our standard of living. But he will find compensatory comfort in thinking of our legal system as undeveloped and of common lawyers as relatively uncultured people. Failure to take this attitude of some civil lawyers toward common

3

lawyers into account can result in misunderstanding and difficulty in communication. One of the purposes of this book is to enable us to understand the origin of this attitude, and incidentally to show how it is, in some ways, a justified one.

The date commonly used to mark the beginning of the common law tradition is A.D. 1066, when the Normans defeated the defending natives at Hastings and conquered England. If we accept that date, the common law tradition is slightly over 900 years old. It is sobering to recall that when the *Corpus Juris Civilis* of Justinian (discussed below) was published in Constantinople in A.D. 533, the civil law tradition, of which it is an important part, was already older than the common law is today. As a result of the remarkable expansion and development of the British Empire during the age of colonialism and empire, however, the common law was very widely distributed. It is today the legal tradition in force in Great Britain, Ireland, the United States, Canada, Australia, and New Zealand, and has had substantial influence on the law of many nations in Asia and Africa.

The socialist law tradition is generally said to have originated at the time of the October Revolution. Before that event, the dominant legal tradition in the Russian Empire was the civil law. One intention of the Soviet revolutionaries was to abolish the bourgeois civil law system and substitute a new socialist legal order. The actual effect of their reform was to impose certain principles of socialist ideology on existing civil law systems and on the civil law tradition. Under the influence of the Soviet Union and Marxist thought, similar legal changes have taken place in those states of Eastern Europe (and in other countries, such as Cuba) that were parts of the civil law tradition before they became socialist states. The result is a young, vigorous legal tradition that still displays its essentially hybrid nature.

The socialist attitude is that all law is an instrument of economic and social policy, and that the common law and civil law traditions basically reflect a capitalistic, bourgeois, imperialist, exploitative society, economy, and government. Socialists see our legal system as incorporating and perpetuating a set of goals and ideals that they regard as socially and economically unjust. At the same time, the common law appears to a Soviet lawyer to be unsystematic and undeveloped, in

4

comparison with carefully drawn Soviet legislation that builds on the civil law tradition of system and of order. Finally, to a socialist lawyer, both the civil law and common law traditions are subject to criticism because they embody but do not clearly state their ideologies. Such a lawyer sees our legal systems as devices by which bourgeois ideals are concealed in ostensibly neutral legal forms, which are then used to exploit the proletariat.

The fact that these three legal traditions are all of European origin should give us pause. There are, of course, many other legal traditions in today's world, and new ones are forming. The dominance of the three traditions of which we have spoken is the direct result of Western European imperialism in earlier centuries and Soviet imperialism in this century (just as the dominance of Roman law in an earlier age was a product of Roman imperialism).

Thus there are many important nations that cannot be included in any one of these three major legal traditions. It is generally thought, for example, that even in Western Europe the Scandinavian legal systems are a thing apart from both the civil law and common law traditions. A large part of the world, particularly in North Africa, but also elsewhere in the Middle East and in Asia, is within the orbit of the Moslem legal tradition, and other religiously oriented legal traditions have substantial influence in other parts of the world. In much of Africa and in many parts of Asia, indigenous legal traditions, often restricted to relatively small geographic areas or tribal groups, are in existence. Most of these have experienced or are experiencing some contact with major legal systems from other parts of the world, and the result frequently is an unstable state of coexistence whose ultimate outcome is not yet apparent. Outstanding examples are India, with its peculiar combination of Hindu law, other native legal influences, and the common law of England (with much of the English law put into the form of systematically codified legislation of a sort that was never introduced into England). Another interesting example is Japan, which in an earlier period received the civil law tradition and the German codes and which later, during the post–World War II occupation period, came under common law influence, particularly in its public law. Both the civil law and common law traditions, to the ex-

tent that they are in force in Japan, are of course imposed on a prior legal tradition that retains some force but is in no way related to either the civil law or the common law.

But these are not our subject; nor are the common law and the socialist law our subject. The purpose of this book is to say something understandable to the educated general reader about the oldest, most widely distributed, and most influential tradition of all, the civil law.

## II

# ROMAN CIVIL LAW, CANON LAW,
# AND COMMERCIAL LAW

WE HAVE been discussing the civil law tradition as though it were homogeneous. Now we must face the unhappy fact that it is really not that simple. The civil law tradition is a composite of several distinct sub-traditions, with separate origins and developments in different periods of history. In this and the next few chapters these sub-traditions will be described under the following headings: Roman civil law, canon law, commercial law, the revolution, and legal science. A brief discussion of each of them provides a convenient way of summarizing the historical development of the civil law tradition and indicating something of the complexity of that tradition.

The oldest sub-tradition is directly traceable to the Roman law as compiled and codified under Justinian in the sixth century A.D. It includes the law of persons, the family, inheritance, property, torts, unjust enrichment, and contracts, and the remedies by which interests falling within these categories are judicially protected. Although the rules actually in force have changed, often drastically, since 533, the first three books of the Institutes of Justinian (Of Persons, Of Things, Of Obligations) and the major nineteenth-century civil codes all deal with substantially the same sets of problems and relationships, and the substantive area they cover is what a civil lawyer calls "civil law." The belief that this group of subjects is a related body of law that constitutes the fundamental content of the legal system is deeply rooted in Europe and the other parts of the world that have received the civil law tradition, and it is one of the principal distinguishing marks of what common lawyers call the civil law system. The expansion of governmental activity and the increasing importance of public law have not seriously altered this outlook. "Civil law" is still fundamental law to most civil lawyers. Hence a problem of terminology. Common lawyers use the term "civil law" to refer to the entire legal system in nations

falling within the civil law tradition. But the legal terminology of lawyers within such a jurisdiction uses "civil law" to refer to that portion of the legal system just described. The problem will be dealt with in this book by using the term "Roman civil law" to refer to this part of the law.

Justinian, a Roman emperor residing in Constantinople, had two principal motivations when he ordered the preparation, under the guidance of the jurist Tribonian, of what is now called the *Corpus Juris Civilis*. First, he was a reactionary: he considered the contemporary Roman law decadent; he sought to rescue the Roman legal system from several centuries of deterioration and restore it to its former purity and grandeur. Second, he was a codifier: the mass of authoritative and quasi-authoritative material had become so great, and included so many refinements and different points of view, that it seemed desirable to Justinian to eliminate that which was wrong, obscure, or repetitive, to resolve conflicts and doubts, and to organize what was worth retaining into some systematic form. In particular, Justinian was concerned about the great number, length, and variety of commentaries and treatises written by legal scholars (called jurisconsults). He sought both to abolish the authority of all but the greatest of the jurisconsults of the classical period and to make it unnecessary for any more commentaries or treatises to be written.

On publication of the *Corpus Juris Civilis*, Justinian forbade any further reference to the works of jurisconsults. Those of their works that he approved were included in the *Corpus Juris Civilis*, and henceforward reference was to be made to it, rather than to the original authorities. He also forbade the preparation of any commentaries on his compilation itself. In other words, he sought to abolish all prior law except that included in the *Corpus Juris Civilis*, and he took the view that what was in his compilation would be adequate for the solution of legal problems without the aid of further interpretation or commentary by legal scholars. He was able to make his prohibition against citation of the original authorities more effective by having some of the manuscripts of their work that had been collected by Tribonian burned. The prohibition against citation to works not included in the *Corpus Juris Civilis* effectively destroyed an even greater

amount of material, because it naturally diminished interest in pre-serving and copying the works of the jurisconsults who had produced them. (These two influences have, understandably, complicated the work of persons interested in studying the pre-Justinian Roman law.) His command that there be no commentaries on the compilation was less effective, however, and was disregarded during his lifetime.

The *Corpus Juris Civilis* of Justinian was not restricted to Roman civil law. It included much that had to do with the power of the emperor, the organization of the empire, and a variety of other matters that lawyers today would classify as public law. But the part of Justinian's compilation that deals with Roman civil law is the part that has been the object of the most intensive study and has become the basis of the legal systems of the civil law world. Other parts of Justinian's compilation have been less carefully studied and used because they have seemed to be less applicable to the problems of other peoples and governments in other times and places. In any event, the part of the *Corpus Juris Civilis* that is devoted to Roman civil law is much the larger part.

With the fall of the Roman Empire, the *Corpus Juris Civilis* fell into disuse. Cruder, less sophisticated versions of the Roman civil law were applied by the invaders to the peoples of the Italian peninsula. The invaders also brought with them their own Germanic legal customs, which, under their rule that the law of a person's nationality followed him wherever he went, were applied to themselves but not to those they had conquered. Even so, a fusion of some Germanic tribal laws with indigenous Roman legal institutions did begin to take place in parts of Italy, southern France, and the Iberian peninsula. Over the centuries this produced what Europeans still refer to as a "vulgarized" or "barbarized" Roman law, which is today of interest primarily to legal historians.

As light returned to Europe, as Europeans regained control of the Mediterranean Sea, and as that extraordinary period of feverish in-tellectual and artistic rebirth called the Renaissance began, an intellectual and scholarly interest in law reappeared. What civil lawyers commonly refer to as "the revival of Roman law" is generally conceded to have had its beginning in Bologna, Italy, late in the eleventh

9

century. It was at Bologna that the first modern European university appeared, and law was a major object of study. But the law that was studied was not the barbarized Roman law that had been in force under the Germanic invaders. Nor was it the body of rules enacted or customarily followed by local towns, merchants' guilds, or petty sovereigns. The law studied was the *Corpus Juris Civilis* of Justinian.

There were several reasons for this attention to the *Corpus Juris Civilis* and neglect of other available bodies of law. First, the conception of a Holy Roman Empire was very strong and real in twelfth-century Italy. Justinian was thought of as a Holy Roman Emperor, and his *Corpus Juris Civilis* was treated as imperial legislation. As such it had the authority of both the pope and the temporal emperor behind it. This made it far superior in force and range of applicability to the legislation of a local prince, the regulations of a guild, or local custom. Second, the jurists recognized the high intellectual quality of the *Corpus Juris Civilis*. They saw that this work, which they called "written reason," was superior to the barbarized compilations that had come into use under the Germanic invader. The *Corpus Juris Civilis* carried not only the authority of the pope and the emperor, but also the authority of an obviously superior civilization and intelligence.

Within a short time, Bologna and the other universities of northern Italy became the legal center of the Western world. Men came from all over Europe to study the law as taught in the Italian universities. The law studied was the *Corpus Juris Civilis*, and the common language of study was Latin. There was a succession of schools of thought about the proper way to study and explain the *Corpus Juris Civilis*. Of special prominence, for both their views of the law and their styles of scholarship, were the groups of scholars known as the Glossators and the Commentators. They produced an immense literature, which itself became the object of study and discussion and came to carry great authority. Those who had studied in Bologna returned to their nations and established universities where they also taught and studied the law of the *Corpus Juris Civilis* according to the style of the Glossators and Commentators. In this way, the Roman civil law and the works of the Glossators and Commentators became the basis of a common law of Europe, which is actually called the jus commune by legal historians.

There was a common body of law and of writing about law, a common legal language, and a common method of teaching and scholarship.

With the rise of the nation-state and the growth of the concept of national sovereignty, particularly from the fifteenth century on, and with the demise of the Holy Roman Empire as anything but a fiction, the age of the jus commune—of a common law of Europe—waned, and the period of national law began. In some parts of Europe (e.g. Germany), the Roman civil law and the writings of the Bolognese scholars were formally "received" as binding law. (Civil lawyers use the term "reception" to sum up the process by which the nation-states of the civil law world came to include the jus commune in their national legal systems.) In other parts of Europe the reception was less formal; the *Corpus Juris Civilis* and the works of the Glossators and Commentators were received because of their value as customary law or because of their appeal as an intellectually superior system. But, by one means or another, the Roman civil law was received throughout a large part of Western Europe, in the nations that are now the home of the civil law tradition.

Eventually, in the nineteenth century, the principal states of Western Europe adopted civil codes (as well as other codes), of which the French Code Napoléon of 1804 is the archetype. The subject matter of these civil codes was almost identical with the subject matter of the first three books of the *Institutes* of Justinian and the jus commune of medieval Europe. The principal concepts were Roman and medieval common law in nature, and the organization and conceptual structure were similar. A European or Latin American civil code of today clearly demonstrates the influence of Roman law and its medieval revival. Roman civil law epitomizes the oldest, most continuously and thoroughly studied, and (in the opinion of civil lawyers) most basic part of the civil law tradition.

The second oldest component of the civil law tradition is the canon law of the Roman Catholic Church. This body of law and procedure was developed by the Church for its own governance and to regulate the rights and obligations of its communicants. Just as the Roman civil law was the universal law of the temporal empire, directly associated with the authority of the emperor, so the canon law was the uni-

versal law of the spiritual domain, directly associated with the authority of the pope. Each had its own sphere of application, and a separate set of courts existed for each: the civil courts for Roman civil law and the ecclesiastical courts for canon law. There was, however, a tendency toward overlapping jurisdiction, and before the Reformation it was common to find ecclesiastical courts exercising civil jurisdiction, particularly in family law and succession matters, as well as jurisdiction over certain types of crimes. The canon law had its beginnings early in the Christian era and has a fascinating history, including forged documents treated for centuries as though they were genuine. Various collections and arrangements of canon law materials were assembled, and by the time of the Bolognese revival there was a substantial body of written canon law available for study.

The study of canon law came to be joined with the study of the Roman civil law in the Italian universities, and the degree conferred on a student who had completed the full course of study was Juris Utriusque Doctor, or Doctor of Both Laws, referring to the civil law and the canon law. The J.U.D. degree is still granted in some universities in the civil law world.) Because the two were studied together in the Italian universities, there was a tendency for them to influence each other; and the canon law, as well as the Roman civil law, helped in the formation of the jus commune that was subsequently received by the European states. Canon law influenced the jus commune mainly in the areas of family law and succession (both parts of the Roman civil law), criminal law, and the law of procedure. By the time the ecclesiastical courts of Europe were deprived of their civil jurisdiction, many substantive and procedural principles and institutions they had developed had been adopted by the civil courts themselves.

This Roman civil law–canon law jus commune was the generally applicable law of Europe. There was also, of course, a great amount of local law, some of it customary and some in the form of legislation by princes, lords, towns, or communes. In general, such law was regarded as exceptional in nature and of only local interest. The attention of the legal scholar was focused on the jus commune, rather than on local variations. Still, local law had some effect on the development of the jus commune. Many of the most important law teachers and scholars

were also practicing lawyers in constant contact with the law in action. What they saw of customary and local law, particularly in fields such as criminal law, where Roman law was undeveloped or considered inapplicable, helped form their ideas about the jus commune. At the same time their scholarly bent and their conviction of the superiority of Roman civil law strongly affected the development of local law. The two tended to converge along lines favored by the scholars.

The reception of the jus commune in European nations eventually aroused a nationalistic concern for the identification and preservation —and in some cases the glorification—of indigenous legal institutions. The *coutumes* of the various French regions generally classified as the *pays de droit coutumier* (regions of customary law)— in contrast to those regions generally classified as *pays de droit écrit* (regions of written law), where Roman law was the dominant influence—became a source of national pride and scholarly interest during the Revolution and afterward, when the law was codified. In the codification an effort was made to include institutions from the *coutumes* in the new centralized legal order. In Germany a dispute arose during the preparatory work of codification between the so-called "Germanists" and "Romanists," and the draft of a civil code originally proposed for unified Germany was rejected because of the opposition of the Germanists. Their complaint was that the draft was purely Roman in form and substance, to the neglect of native legal institutions, and they were able to force a revision for the purpose of giving the code a more German, less purely Roman, flavor.

In these and other ways, the development of a national legal system in each of the major European nations took on certain characteristics directly traceable to the desire to identify, perpetuate, and glorify indigenous legal institutions. This tendency is indeed one of the main reasons for the substantial differences that exist between contemporary civil law systems. But what binds such nations together is that these indigenous legal institutions have been combined with the form and substance of Roman civil law, under the influence of the jus commune. The Roman influence is very great; the native legal contribution, while substantial, is generally of subsidiary importance. It does not go to such matters as basic legal attitudes and notions, or to the organization

and style of the legal order. These are drawn from the older, more fully developed and sophisticated Roman civil law tradition.

The third sub-tradition, after Roman civil law and canon law, is commercial law. Although it is obvious that some form of commercial law is as old as commerce, the commercial law of Western Europe (and also, as it happens, of the common law world) had its principal development in Italy at the time of the Crusades, when European commerce regained dominance in the Mediterranean area. Italian merchants formed guilds and established rules for the conduct of commercial affairs. Medieval Italian towns became commercial centers, and the rules developed within these towns—particularly Amalfi, Genoa, Pisa, and Venice—were influential in the development of commercial law. Unlike Roman civil law and canon law, which were bookish and dominated by scholars, commercial law was the pragmatic creation of practical men engaged in commerce. Interpretation and application of the commercial law went on in commercial courts, in which the judges were merchants. The needs of commerce and the interests of merchants, not the compilation of Justinian or those of the canonists, were the main sources of the law.

The commercial law that developed out of the activities of the guilds and of the maritime cities soon became international in character. It became a common commercial law that penetrated throughout the commercial world, even into areas, such as England, where the Roman civil law had met with resistance. This common commercial law of Europe was later received by the nation-states, and eventually was incorporated into the commercial codes adopted throughout the civil law world in the eighteenth and nineteenth centuries.

These three sub-traditions within the civil law tradition—Roman civil law, canon law, and commercial law—are the principal historical sources of the concepts, institutions, and procedures of most of the private law and procedural law, and much of the criminal law of modern civil law systems. In modern form, as affected by revolutionary law and legal science (described in the next few chapters), they are embodied in the five basic codes typically found in a civil law jurisdiction: the civil code, the commercial code, the code of civil procedure, the penal code, and the code of criminal procedure.

# III

# THE REVOLUTION

THREE OF the five principal sub-traditions of the civil law tradition —Roman civil law, canon law, and commercial law—are, as we have seen, the historical sources of much of the law embodied in the five basic codes in force in most civil law jurisdictions. The reader will observe that much of public law, particularly constitutional law and administrative law, is conspicuously absent from this listing. The reason is that the public law in contemporary civil law nations is in large part a product of a revolution that took place in the West in the century beginning with 1776. This movement, which affected most Western nations, included such dramatic events as the American and French revolutions, the Italian Risorgimento, the series of wars of independence that liberated the nations of South and Central America, the unification of Germany under Bismarck, and the liberation of Greece after centuries of Turkish domination.

But these events were themselves products of a more fundamental intellectual revolution. Certain long-established patterns of thought about government and the individual were finally overcome, and newer ways of thinking about man, society, the economy, and the state took their place. Even in parts of the West that escaped violent revolutions (e.g. England), these newer ideas came to prevail. It is in this intellectual revolution that we find the main sources of public law in the civil law tradition. Although a careful historical investigation could undoubtedly trace the origin of a number of contemporary governmental institutions to legal materials that preceded this revolution, the fact is that the guiding spirit of European public law and many of the concepts and institutions in which it is expressed are of modern origin, and do not have deep roots in the Roman or medieval periods of European history.

The effect of the revolution was not, however, limited to public law. It also had a profound influence on the form, the method of applica-

tion, and, to a lesser extent, the content of the basic codes derived from Roman and jus commune sources. The intellectual revolution produced a new way of thinking about law that had important consequences for the organization and administration of the legal system and for rules of substantive and procedural law.

One of the principal driving intellectual forces of the revolution was what has since come to be called secular natural law. It was based on certain ideas about man's nature that find expression in the American Declaration of Independence and in the French Declaration of the Rights of Man and of the Citizen. All men, so the reasoning goes, are created equal. They have certain natural rights to property, to liberty, to life. The proper function of government is to recognize and secure these rights and to ensure equality among men. Government should be carried on by elected representatives. And so on.

The surviving institutions of feudalism, which conferred social status and public office on the basis of land ownership, were clearly inconsistent with these ideas. So were aristocracies of other kinds, based on considerations other than the ownership of land, such as the aristocracy of the robe. Before the French Revolution, judicial offices were regarded as property that one could buy, sell, and leave to one's heir on one's death. Montesquieu himself inherited such an office, held it for a decade, and sold it. The judges were an aristocratic group who supported the landed aristocracy against the peasants and the urban working and middle classes, and against the centralization of governmental power in Paris. When the Revolution came, the aristocracy fell, and with it fell the aristocracy of the robe.

A second tenet of the intellectual revolution was the separation of governmental powers. A number of writers, notably Montesquieu in his *Spirit of the Laws* and Rousseau in *The Social Contract*, had persuasively argued the fundamental importance to rational democratic government of establishing and maintaining a separation of governmental powers, and in particular of keeping the legislative and executive separate from the judicial power. This fear of unchecked judicial power did not exist in the United States either before or after the American Revolution. The system of checks and balances that has emerged in the United States places no special emphasis on isolating

the judiciary, and it proceeds from a philosophy different from that which produced the sharp separation of powers customarily encountered in the civil law world. It is important to emphasize this point and to understand why this was the case.

In France the judicial aristocracy were targets of the Revolution not only because of their tendency to identify with the landed aristocracy, but also because of their failure to distinguish very clearly between applying law and making law. As a result of these failings, efforts by the Crown to unify the kingdom and to enforce relatively enlightened and progressive legislative reforms had frequently been frustrated. The courts refused to apply the new laws, interpreted them contrary to their intent, or hindered the attempts of officials to administer them. Montesquieu and others developed the theory that the only sure way of preventing abuses of this kind was first to separate the legislative and executive from the judicial power, and then to regulate the judiciary carefully to ensure that it restricted itself to applying the law made by the legislature and did not interfere with public officials performing their administrative functions.

In the United States and England, on the contrary, there was a different kind of judicial tradition, one in which judges had often been a progressive force on the side of the individual against the abuse of power by the ruler, and had played an important part in the centralization of governmental power and the destruction of feudalism. The fear of judicial lawmaking and of judicial interference in administration did not exist. On the contrary, the power of the judges to shape the development of the common law was a familiar and welcome institution. The judiciary was not a target of the American Revolution in the way that it was in France.

The age was also the Age of Reason. Rationalism was a dominant intellectual force. It was assumed that reason controlled men's activities and that all obstacles would fall before the proper exercise of careful thought by intelligent men. The subconscious had not yet been discovered, and the power of irrational forces in history was not yet recognized. It was optimistically assumed that existing laws and institutions could be repealed and new ones, rationally derived from unimpeachable first principles, put in their place.

The emphasis on the rights of man in the revolutionary period produced statements about individual liberty of the sort found in our Declaration of Independence and in the French Declaration of the Rights of Man and of the Citizen. There was, however, a very important difference. Feudalism (in the general, nontechnical sense of the term as it was used by many European and Latin American revolutionaries) had survived in Europe and Latin America in a form that kept alive many of the social injustices inherent in its origins, whereas in the American colonies, legal institutions of undeniably feudal origin had already been deprived of much of their ability to produce the kind of social and economic evils that characterized feudal societies. As a consequence the intellectual revolution in the civil law world was more intensely antifeudal in orientation than it was in the United States. The emphasis on the right of a man to own property and on the obligation of the law to protect his ownership was in part a reaction against dependent tenure under feudalism. The emphasis on a man's right to conduct his own affairs and to move laterally and vertically in society was a reaction against the tendency under feudalism to fix a man in a place and status. The revolution became, to use Sir Henry Maine's famous phrase, an instrument for the transition "from status to contract." The result was an exaggerated emphasis on private property and liberty of contract, similar in effect to the exaggerated individualism of nineteenth-century England and America. But the reaction in the civil law world carried a special antifeudal flavor.

The revolution was also a great step along the path toward glorification of the secular state. Henceforward the temporal allegiance of the individual would be owed primarily to the state. Feudal obligations and relationships were abolished. Religious obligations lost most of their remaining legal importance. The ecclesiastical courts lost what little remained of their temporal jurisdiction. Family relationships were now defined and regulated by law (i.e. by the state). Local governmental autonomies were abolished; guilds and corporations were deprived of regulatory power. Separate legal traditions were merged into a single body of national law. The legal universe, formerly very complicated, was suddenly simplified: henceforward it would in theory be inhabited only by the individual and the monolithic state.

Nationalism was another aspect of the glorification of the state. The objective was a national legal system that would express national ideals and the unity of the nation's culture. Such a national law should be expressed in a national language and should incorporate national legal institutions and concepts. The authority (but not the content) of the jus commune was rejected; a common law of the civil law world was now history. In the future all law would be national law, and variation from the jus commune was not only accepted, but valued as evidence of national genius and identity.

Thus the revolution was composed of such intellectual forces as natural rights, the separation of powers, rationalism, antifeudalism, bourgeois liberalism, statism, and nationalism. These are all respectable enough as ideas or points of view, so long as they are kept in proportion. But during and following the revolution a general atmosphere of exaggeration prevailed (as is typical of revolutionary movements). The hated past was painted in excessively dark colors. The objectives of the revolution were idealized and the possibility of their accomplishment assumed. The problems in the way of reform were ignored or oversimplified. Ideological passion displaced reason; revolutionary ideas became dogmas; the revolution became utopian.

In France in particular, just as in the Soviet Union after the October Revolution, the utopian flavor was very strong. It profoundly affected the revolutionary reforms in France, and since the revolutionary law of France has been extremely influential outside of France, the legal systems in many parts of the civil law world show the effects both of the utopianism that characterized the French Revolution and of reactions against it. The emphasis on separation of powers led to a separate system of administrative courts, inhibited the adoption of judicial review of legislation, and limited the judge to a relatively minor role in the legal process. The theory of natural rights led to an exaggerated emphasis on individual rights of property and contract and to an oversharp distinction between public and private law. Glorification of the state, nationalism, and rationalism combined to produce a peculiar civil law theory of what law is and to determine the form and style of the basic codes.

# IV

## THE SOURCES OF LAW

IN THE PERIOD of revolutionary change we have been discussing, the social and economic injustices of the old order were brought into direct conflict with the desire for egalitarianism. The awkward, highly decentralized, inefficient structure of feudal government fell before the need for a more efficient, centralized governmental system—the modern nation-state. Both in order to bring about this kind of transformation and in order to consolidate the accomplishments of the revolution, an ideology was needed, and nationalism—the ideology of the state—met this need. And if nationalism was the prevailing ideology, sovereignty was the basic premise of its legal expression.

The concept of sovereignty had existed for several centuries. Its development as a legal concept can be traced to the work of certain Europeans, notably Hugo Grotius, who are often called the "fathers of international law." These scholars employed sovereignty as a fundamental concept for ordering international affairs between nations. During the period of colonialism and the foundation of empires, they built a school of international law that both supported the claims and attempted to control the conduct of the colonial and empire-building powers. During the emergence of the nation-state the same concept was put to new, somewhat different uses.

Another dimension of the movement toward state positivism was provided by the secular character of the European revolution. Although there were variations in form and degree from nation to nation, the idea that law was of divine origin—whether expressed directly, as in divine (i.e. scriptural) law, or expressed indirectly through the nature of man as created by God, as in Roman Catholic natural law—now lost most of its remaining vitality. Formal respect might still be paid to the deity in the lawmaking process (as, for example, in the American Declaration of Independence), but henceforward the operating theory was that the ultimate lawmaking power

20

lay in the state. Roman Catholic natural law had lost its power to control the prince. Secular natural law, while providing many of the ideas
that were the intellectual fuel of the revolution, was ineffectual as a
control on the activity of the state. It was backed by no organization
and had no sanctioning power. The perennial controversy between
natural lawyers and legal positivists (familiar to all students of legal
philosophy) thus was decisively resolved, for operational purposes at
least, in favor of the positivists. Consequently, although this debate
still goes on, it has had a distinctly academic flavor since the emergence of the modern state. All Western states are positivistic.

The emergence of the modern nation-state destroyed the legal unity
provided by common acceptance of the Roman-canonic jus commune
in feudal Europe. The jus commune, associated in many minds with
the concept of the Holy Roman Empire, was a law that transcended
the diversities of local tribes, communities, and nations. With the decay
of feudalism, the advent of the Reformation, and the consequent weak-
ening of the authority of the Holy Roman Empire, the centralized
monarchy began to emerge as the principal claimant to men's loyalty.
The centralized state stood in opposition both to the medieval autonomy of classes and lands commonly associated with feudalism and to
every kind of power outside the state. The state tended to become the
unique source of law, claiming sovereignty for itself both internally
and internationally. Thus national legal systems began to replace the
jus commune, which became a subordinate or supplementary law.
Roman law itself was quoted as providing, in the maxim *quod principi
placuit habet vigorem* (the prince's pleasure is law), justification for
the legal autonomy of the state that led eventually to its displacement
in favor of national legal systems. The authority of the prince replaced
that of the jus commune. The content of national law might continue
to be drawn largely from the jus commune, but its authority came
from the state.

So the age of absolute sovereignty began. Where the jus commune
was formally received, as it was in part of Germany, it was by the will
of the prince, and its continued force within the state also depended
in theory on his will. But where, as in most of Europe, there was no
formal reception of the Roman law, the process of building a national

law (usually in the national language) took place under conditions and on the basis of assumptions that presaged European legal positivism. The legislative act was subject to no authority, temporal or spiritual, superior to the state, nor was it subject to any limitation from within the state (such as local or customary law). From a time when lawmaking was distributed along a spectrum running from the local lord or town council through the emperor and the Universal Church, the West had moved to lawmaking at only one point: the centralized nation-state. Sovereignty had two faces, an outer face that excluded any law of external origin and an inner face that excluded any law of local or customary origin.

It is important to understand that state positivism was much more sharply and consciously emphasized on the Continent than it was in England during this period of revolutionary change. One reason, of course, was the milder, more gradual, and more evolutionary nature of the English revolution. In England many of the forms of feudalism were retained, while their substance was transformed. The trappings of an established church survived, while that church's influence on the form and content of lawmaking diminished to the vanishing point. Most important of all, the indigenous common law of England, which had developed along lines quite different from those taken by the jus commune on the Continent, was not rejected in the interest of statism, nationalism, positivism, and sovereignty. On the contrary, the common law of England was a positive force in the emergence of England as a nation-state, and was vigorously embraced as evidence of national identity and national genius. On the Continent the revolution seemed to require a rejection of the old legal order; in England it seemed to require acceptance and even glorification of it. The implications of this difference for the attitudes toward codification in the civil law and common law worlds are obvious. On the Continent, where it was thought necessary to reject the jus commune, it was natural that new legal systems were codified; in England, where it was thought necessary to retain the common law, no need for codification was felt.

On the Continent the rejection of the old order proceeded along the lines indicated by a vision of the world as properly organized into secular, positivistic nation-states. Consequently, the natural law of the

Roman Catholic Church, like other externally derived theories of law and justice, and the canon law, like other external bodies of rules and institutions, could not have effect as law within the state. The Western school of international law, which is based on a kind of absolute sovereignty of the state that permits it to be bound only when it agrees to be, treated even accepted principles of international law as operative within the state only if the state itself decided that they should be. The law produced by international organizations and the obligations of members of such organizations again affected the state only if it had agreed to be subject to them. The laws of one state could only be enforced within another state if the latter chose to permit their enforcement. A judgment rendered by a court of one state would or would not be enforced by the courts of another state at the latter's option. The outward face of state positivism was thus uniform and unbroken: nothing outside the state could make law effective on or within the state without the state's consent.

The inner face of the school of state positivism was equally unbroken. Only the state had lawmaking power, and hence no individual or group within the state could produce law. The ability of individuals to bind themselves by contracts and of the members of organizations to adopt effective rules governing their internal relations did not give them lawmaking power. These were considered to be private arrangements, which had legal effect only to the extent that the state chose to recognize and enforce them. Books and articles written by scholars (although much more influential than legal scholarship in common law countries, as will be explained in a subsequent chapter) also were not law, for the same reasons.

Thus state positivism, as expressed in the dogma of the absolute external and internal sovereignty of the state, led to a state monopoly on lawmaking. Revolutionary emphasis on the strict separation of powers demanded that only specifically designated organs of the state be entitled to make law. According to that doctrine, the legislative and judicial powers of the government were different in kind; in order to prevent abuse, they had to be very sharply separated from each other. The legislative power is by definition the lawmaking power, and hence only the legislature could make law. As the only representa-

tive, directly elected branch of the government, the legislature alone could respond to the popular will. Some of the consequences of this dogma for the civil law judge will be discussed in the next chapter. For now it need only be said that the familiar common law doctrine of *stare decisis*—i.e. the doctrine that similar cases should be decided similarly—is obviously inconsistent with the separation of powers as formulated in civil law countries, and is therefore rejected by the civil law tradition. Judicial decisions are not law.

What, then, was law? The basic answer, which is the essence of legislative positivism, is that only statutes enacted by the legislative power could be law. However, it was common in civil law nations for the prince to have lawmaking power within certain limits. After the various Western revolutions, such decrees derived their force as law not from any inherent lawmaking power in the executive, but from the delegation of lawmaking power to the executive by the legislature, which was the sole repository of that power. By the same reasoning, the legislature could delegate the power to promulgate regulations having the force of law to administrate organs of the government. Such delegated legislative and administrative regulations were effective as law only within the limits of the power delegated by the legislature. Anything that exceeded that power would be "illegal," and consequently not law.

In addition to statutes (including legislation promulgated by the executive under delegated powers) and administrative regulations, nations within the civil law tradition still commonly recognize a third source of law, called custom. Where a person acts in accordance with custom under the assumption that it represents the law, his action will be accepted as legal in many civil law jurisdictions, so long as there is no applicable statute or regulation to the contrary. The amount of writing on custom as law in civil law jurisdictions is immense, far out of proportion to its actual importance as law. The main reason for so much writing (in addition to the importance of custom as a source of law in the earlier history of the civil law tradition) is the need to justify treating as law something that is not created by the legislative power of the state. To give custom the force of law would appear to violate the dogma of state positivism (only the state can make law)

and the dogma of sharp separation of powers (within the state only the legislature can make law). Some very sophisticated theories have been developed to explain away this apparent inconsistency. Meanwhile the importance of custom as a source of law is slight and decreasing.

The result of all this is that the accepted theory of sources of law in the civil law tradition recognizes only statutes, regulations, and custom as sources of law. This listing is exclusive. It is also arranged in descending order of authority. A statute prevails over a contrary regulation. Both a statute and a regulation prevail over an inconsistent custom. This may all seem very technical and of dubious importance, but in fact it is basic to our understanding of the civil law tradition, since the function of the judge within that tradition is to interpret and to apply "the law" as it is technically defined in his jurisdiction. Both state positivism and the dogma of separation of powers require that the judge resort only to "the law" in deciding cases. It is assumed that whatever the problem that may come before him, the judge will be able to find some form of law to apply—whether a statute, a regulation, or an applicable custom. He cannot turn to books and articles by legal scholars or to prior judicial decisions for the law.

This dogmatic conception of what law is, like many other implications of the dogmas of the revolutionary period, has been eroded by time and events. Perhaps the most spectacular innovation has been the strong movement toward constitutionalism, with its emphasis on the functional rigidity, and hence the superiority as a source of law, of written constitutions. Such constitutions, by eliminating the power of the legislature to amend by ordinary legislative action, impair the legislature's monopoly on lawmaking. They insert a new element into the hierarchy of sources of law, which now must read "constitution, legislation, regulations, and custom." In addition, if a court can decide that a statute is void because it is in conflict with the constitution, the dogma of sharp separation of legislative from judicial power is impaired. Judicial review of the constitutionality of legislative action exists, in one form or another, in many civil law nations that have rigid constitutions. Another complicating factor is the inclusion of the initiative and the referendum in the constitutions of some civil

law countries; this necessarily involves the transfer of some lawmaking power from the legislature to the people, and further weakens the position of the legislature as the sole source of law. The growth of international and supranational organizations, and the trend in Europe and Latin America toward the transfer of some sovereignty to such organizations, further weakens the traditional theory.

These and other modern tendencies have been noted by scholars, who often recognize their implications for the orthodox theory of sources of law, but they do not seriously impair the more generally prevailing view of what law is. To the average judge, lawyer, or law student in France or Argentina, the traditional theory of sources of law represents the basic truth. It is a part of his ideology.

In the common law world, on the other hand, a world less compelled by the peculiar history and the rationalist dogmas of the French Revolution, quite different attitudes prevail. The common law of England, an unsystematic accretion of statutes, judicial decisions, and customary practices, is thought of as the major source of law. It has deep historic dimensions and is not the product of a conscious revolutionary attempt to make or to restate the applicable law at a moment in history. There is no systematic, hierarchical theory of sources of law: legislation, of course, is law, but so are other things, including judicial decisions. In formal terms the relative authority of statutes, regulations, and judicial decisions might run in roughly that order, but in practice such formulations tend to lose their neatness and their importance. Common lawyers tend to be much less rigorous about such matters than civil lawyers. The attitudes that led France to adopt the metric system, decimal currency, legal codes, and a rigid theory of sources of law, all in the space of a few years, are still basically alien to the common law tradition.

# V

## CODES AND CODIFICATION

ONE OFTEN hears it said, sometimes by people who should know better, that civil law systems are codified statutory systems, whereas the common law is uncodified and is based in large part on judicial decisions. The purpose of this chapter is to indicate the extent to which this observation oversimplifies and misrepresents, and at the same time the extent to which it expresses an important set of basic differences between the two legal traditions.

The distinction between legislative and judicial production of law can be misleading. There is probably at least as much legislation in force in a typical American state as there is in a typical European or Latin American nation. As in a civil law nation, legislation validly enacted in the United States is the law, which the judges are expected to interpret and apply in the spirit in which it was enacted. The authority of legislation is superior to that of judicial decisions; statutes supersede contrary judicial decisions (constitutional questions aside), but not vice versa. The amount of legislation and the degree of authority of legislation are not useful criteria for distinguishing civil law systems from common law systems.

Nor is the existence of something called a code a distinguishing criterion. California has more codes than any civil law nation, but California is not a civil law jurisdiction. Codes do exist in most civil law systems, but bodies of systematic legislation covering broad areas of the law and indistinguishable in appearance from European or Latin American codes also exist in a number of common law nations. Conversely, a civil law system need not have codes. Hungary and Greece were civil law countries even before they enacted their civil codes: Hungarian civil law was uncodified until Hungary became a socialist state, and Greece enacted its first civil code after World War II. The code form is not a distinctive identifying mark of a civil law system.

If, however, one thinks of codification not as a form but as the ex-

pression of an ideology, and if one tries to understand that ideology and why it achieves expression in code form, then one can see how it makes sense to talk about codes in comparative law. It is true that California has a number of what are called codes, as do some other states in the United States, and that the Uniform Commercial Code has been adopted in most American jurisdictions. However, although these look like the codes in civil law countries, the underlying ideology —the conception of what a code is and of the functions it should perform in the legal process—is not the same. There is an entirely different ideology of codification at work in the civil law world.

It will be recalled that Justinian, when he promulgated the *Corpus Juris Civilis*, sought to abolish all prior law. Certain elements of the prior legal order were, however, included in the *Corpus Juris Civilis* itself, and were consequently preserved when he promulgated it. Similarly, the French, when they codified their law, repealed all prior law in the areas covered by the codes. Any principles of prior law that were incorporated in the codes received their validity not from their previous existence, but from their incorporation and reenactment in codified form. Justinian and the French codifiers sought to destroy prior law for different but analogous reasons: Justinian sought to reestablish the purer law of an earlier time, the French to establish an entirely new legal order. In both cases, the aims were essentially utopian. Let us look more closely at the utopia of the French codification.

The ideology of the French codification accurately reflects the ideology of the French Revolution. For example, one reason for the attempt to repeal all prior law, and thus limit the effect of law to new legislation, was statism—the glorification of the nation-state. A law that had its origins in an earlier time, before the creation of the state, violated this statist ideal. So did a law that had its origin outside the state—in a European common law, for instance. The nationalism of the time was also an important factor. Much of the prerevolutionary law in France was European rather than French in origin (the jus commune), and was consequently offensive to the rising spirit of French nationalism. At the same time, much that was French (the *coutumes* of the northern regions in particular) now appeared as the

logical object of preservation and glorification. The drive toward a centralized state made it important to bring some unity out of the diversity of legal systems and materials in the French regions. The secular natural law ideal of one law applicable to all Frenchmen pointed the same way.

The rampant rationalism of the time also had an important effect on French codification. Only an exaggerated rationalism can explain the belief that history could be abolished by a repealing statute. Such an attitude is implicit also in the hypothesis that an entirely new legal system, incorporating only certain desirable aspects of the generally undesirable prior legal system, could be created and substituted for the old system. The assumption was that reasoning from basic premises established by the thinkers of the secular natural law school, one could derive a legal system that would meet the needs of the new society and the new government. The legal scholars of the time were, of course, trained in an earlier period, and they found their working legal conceptions, institutions, and processes in the old law. Those who participated in drafting the French codes consequently incorporated a good deal of the prior law and legal learning into them. In this way some continuity with the prior legal culture was retained. This tempered the legal consequences of the French Revolution, but it did not entirely avoid them. For several decades after the enactment of the Code Napoléon (the French Civil Code of 1804), the fiction was stoutly maintained by a large group of French jurists that history was irrelevant to interpretation and application of the code.

As in many Utopias, one of the objectives of the Revolution was to make lawyers unnecessary. There was a desire for a legal system that was simple, nontechnical, and straightforward—one in which the professionalism and the tendency toward technicality and complication commonly blamed on lawyers could be avoided. One way to do this was to state the law clearly and in a straightforward fashion, so that the ordinary citizen could read the law and understand what his rights and obligations were, without having to consult lawyers and go to court. Thus the French Civil Code of 1804 was envisioned as a kind of popular book that could be put on the shelf next to the family Bible.

It would be a handbook for the citizen, clearly organized and stated in straightforward language, that would allow citizens to determine their legal rights and obligations by themselves.

The emphasis on complete separation of powers, with all lawmaking power lodged in a representative legislature, required that the judiciary be denied lawmaking power. Experience with the prerevolutionary courts had made the French wary of judicial lawmaking disguised as interpretation of laws. Therefore some writers argued that judges should be denied even the power to interpret legislation. (The history of this attitude and its subsequent relaxation are described in Chapter VII.) At the same time, however, the judge had to decide every case that came before him. The premises of secular natural law required that justice be available to all Frenchmen; there could be no area for judicial selection or discretion in the exercise of jurisdiction.

But if the legislature alone could make laws and the judiciary could only apply them (or, at a later time, interpret and apply them), such legislation had to be complete, coherent, and clear. If a judge were required to decide a case for which there was no legislative provision, he would in effect make law and thus violate the principle of rigid separation of powers. Hence it was necessary that the legislature draft a code without gaps. Similarly, if there were conflicting provisions in the code, the judge would make law by choosing one rather than another as more applicable to the situation. Hence there could be no conflicting provisions. Finally, if a judge were allowed to decide what meaning to give to an ambiguous provision or an obscure statement, he would again be making law. Hence the code had to be clear.

If insistence on a sharp separation of legislative from judicial power dictated that the codes be complete, coherent, and clear, the prevailing spirit of optimistic rationalism persuaded those in its spell that it was possible to draft complete systematic legislation that would have those characteristics to such a degree that the function of the judge would be limited to selecting the applicable provision of the code and giving it its obvious significance in the context of the case. Actually, the Code Napoléon is not the most extreme example of this type of codification. That dubious honor falls to the Prussian Landrecht of 1794, enacted under Frederick the Great and containing some sixteen thousand de-

tailed provisions setting out precise rules to govern specific "fact situations." The French civil code was drafted by experienced and intelligent jurists who were familiar with the rather spectacular failure of the Prussian attempt to spell it all out. Indeed, if we read the comments of Jean-Etienne-Marie Portalis, one of the most influential of the compilers of the code, we find a constant realistic concern to avoid the extremes of rationalist ideology. Portalis shows us that the code builds on much prerevolutionary law and legal scholarship; and he remarks that the provisions of the code are best thought of as principles or maxims, "féconds en conséquences," to be developed and applied by judges and other jurists.

This kind of professional realism was, however, easily and quickly submerged by the rhetoric of the Revolution and by the excesses of the prevailing rationalism. The code became a victim of the revolutionary ideology, and was uniformly treated as though it were a conscious expression of that ideology, both in France and in the many nations in other parts of the world that were heavily influenced by the French Revolution. Some of the problems that this has created for civil lawyers will be discussed in subsequent chapters.

In contrast to the essentially revolutionary, rationalistic, and nontechnical character of the Code Napoléon, the German Civil Code of 1896 (effective in 1900) was historically oriented, scientific, and professional. A large share of the credit (or blame) for the differences between the German and the French civil codes is owed to Friedrich Karl von Savigny, one of the most famous names in the history of the civil law tradition.

The idea of codification aroused widespread interest in Germany and other parts of Europe and in Latin America during the first part of the nineteenth century. The French code was widely admired and copied, and in the course of time it was proposed that Germany follow France's lead. Savigny prevented this by persuasively arguing a thesis that became very influential in Germany among a group of legal scholars generally referred to as "the historical school." His basic thesis was that it would be wrong for Germany to attempt to devise a civil code by reasoning from principles of secular natural law. In his view, the law of a people was a historically determined product of that

people's development. Consequently, a thorough study of the existing German law and of its historical development was a necessary prelude to proper codification. Since the Roman civil law as interpreted by the medieval Italian scholars had been formally received in Germany some centuries before, a thorough historical study of German law would require a historical study of Roman law and old Germanic law as well as of more recent elements of the contemporary German legal system. Under the influence of Savigny and others of the historical school, many German scholars turned their energies to the intensive study of legal history.

Savigny's idea was that by thoroughly studying the German legal system in its historical context legal scholars would be able to draw from it those historically derived principles that were an essential part of it. These essential features of the law could then be individually studied, studied in relation to other such principles, and eventually systematically restated. The result would be a reconstruction of the historically derived German legal system according to its basic principles and features. This, in turn, would provide the necessary basis for the codification of German law.

The components of the German legal system, in their historical context, came to be thought of by certain successors of Savigny as something like natural data. Just as natural data in biology, chemistry, or physics could be studied in order to determine the more general principles of which they were specific manifestations, so the data of German law could be studied in order to identify and extract from them those inherent principles of the German legal order of which they were specific expressions. Hence the proposed reconstruction of the German legal system was to be a *scientific* reconstruction. (This conception is discussed at greater length in Chapter X.) Finally, the Germans were convinced that it was neither desirable nor possible to rid the world of lawyers. The idea that the law should be clearly and simply stated so that it could be correctly understood and applied by the popular reader was expressly rejected. The German view was that lawyers would be needed, that they would engage in interpreting and applying the law, and that consequently the code they prepared should be responsive to the needs of those trained in the law.

Consequently, the German Civil Code of 1896 is the opposite of revolutionary. It was not intended to abolish prior law and substitute a new legal system; on the contrary, the idea was to codify those principles of German law that would emerge from careful historical study of the German legal system. Instead of trying to discover true principles of law from assumptions about man's nature, as the French did under the influence of secular natural law, the Germans sought to find fundamental principles of German law by scientific study of the data of German law: the existing German legal system in historical context. Rather than a textbook for the layman, the German civil code was thought of as a tool to be used primarily by professionals of the law.

Does this mean that the German civil code and the French civil code are totally dissimilar? It does not. There are differences, and they are important, but some overriding similarities remain. The Germans, like the French, have incorporated a sharp separation of powers into their system of law and government. It is the function of the legislator to make law, and the judge must be prevented from doing so. While displaying a more sophisticated awareness of the difficulty of making a code complete, coherent, and clear, the Germans nevertheless sought to do exactly that, and for the same basic reasons that motivated the French. The German code also served a unifying function, providing a single body of law for the recently unified nation. And like the French code, it thus supported the emergence of the monolithic nation-state.

An entirely different set of ideals and assumptions is associated with the California Civil Code, or with the Uniform Commercial Code as adopted in any American jurisdiction. Even though such codes may look very much like a French or a German code, they are not based on the same ideology, and they do not express anything like the same cultural reality. Where such codes exist, they make no pretense of completeness. The judge is not compelled to find a basis for deciding a given case within the code. Usually, moreover, such codes are not rejections of the past; they do not purport to abolish all prior law in their field, but rather to perfect it and, except where it conflicts with their specific present purposes, to supplement it. Where some

provision of a code or other statute appears to be in possible conflict with a deeply rooted rule of the common law, the tendency will be to interpret the code provision in such a way as to evade the conflict. "Statutes in derogation of the common law," according to a famous judicial quotation, "are strictly construed."

Thus the conservative tendencies of the common law tradition stand in marked contrast to the ideology of revolution from which the spirit of civil law codification emerged. It is this ideology, rather than the form of codification, that helps to bind civil law nations together in a common legal tradition. Like the work of the Glossators and Commentators, which was received together with the *Corpus Juris Civilis* in Europe, the work of the European legal scholars has been adopted, together with the form of European codification, in the civil law nations of Latin America, Asia, and Africa. This work, and the ideology it embodies, is of prime importance to an understanding of the civil law tradition.

# VI

## JUDGES

W E IN THE common law world know what a judge is. He is a culture hero, even something of a father figure. Many of the great
names of the common law are those of judges: Coke, Mansfield, Mar-
shall, Story, Holmes, Brandeis, Cardozo. We know that our legal
tradition was originally created and has grown and developed in the
hands of judges, reasoning closely from case to case and building a
body of law that binds subsequent judges, through the doctrine of
*stare decisis,* to decide similar cases similarly. We know that there is
an abundance of legislation in force, and we recognize that there is a
legislative function. But to us the common law means the law created
and molded by the judges, and we still think (often quite inaccurately)
of legislation as serving a kind of supplementary function. We are
accustomed, in the common law world, to judicial review of administrative action, and in the United States the power of judges to hold
legislation invalid if unconstitutional is accepted without serious question. We know that our judges exercise very broad interpretative
powers, even where the applicable statute or administrative action is
found to be legally valid. We do not like to use such dramatic phrases
as "judicial supremacy" but when pushed to it we admit that this is
a fair description of the common law system, particularly in the United
States.

We also know where our judges come from. We know that they
attend law school and then have successful careers either in private
practice or in government, frequently as district attorneys. They are
appointed or elected to judicial positions on the basis of a variety of
factors, including success in practice, their reputation among their
fellow lawyers, and political influence. Appointment or election to the
bench comes as a kind of crowning achievement relatively late in life.
It is a form of recognition that brings respect and prestige. The judge
is well paid, and if he is among the higher judicial echelons, he will

have secretaries and research assistants. If he sits on the highest court of a state or is high in the federal judiciary, his name may be a household word. His opinions will be discussed in the newspapers and dissected and criticized in the legal periodicals. He is a very important person.

This is what common lawyers mean when they talk about judges. But in the civil law world, a judge is something entirely different. He is a civil servant, a functionary. Although there are important variations, the general pattern is as follows. A judicial career is one of several possibilities open to a student graduating from a university law school. Shortly after graduation, if he wishes to follow a judicial career, he will take a state examination for aspirants to the judiciary and, if successful, will be appointed as a junior judge. Before very long, he will actually be sitting as a judge somewhere low in the hierarchy of courts. In time, he will rise in the judiciary at a rate dependent on some combination of demonstrated ability and seniority. He will receive salary increases according to preestablished schedules, and will belong to an organization of judges that has improvement of judicial salaries, working conditions, and tenure as a principal objective.

Lateral entry into the judiciary is rare. Although provision is made in some civil law jurisdictions for the appointment of distinguished practicing attorneys or professors to high courts, the great majority of judicial offices, even at the highest level, are filled from within the ranks of the professional judiciary. Judges of the high courts receive, and deserve, public respect, but it is the kind of public respect earned and received by persons in high places elsewhere in the civil service.

One of the principal reasons for the quite different status of the civil law judge is the existence of a different judicial tradition in the civil law, beginning in Roman times. The judge (*iudex*) of Rome was not a prominent man of the law. Prior to the Imperial period he was, in effect, a layman discharging an arbitral function by presiding over the settlement of disputes according to formulae supplied by another official, the *praetor*. The *iudex* was not expert in the law and had very limited power. For legal advice he turned to the jurisconsult. Later, during the Imperial period, the adjudication of disputes fell more and more into the hands of public officials who were also learned in the

law, but by that time their principal function was clearly stated to be that of applying the emperor's will. The judge had no inherent law-making power. He was similarly limited in medieval times. One of the grievances against the French judiciary, which seems to have been the target of so many prerevolutionary complaints and postrevolutionary reforms, was that the judges were varying from the traditional Continental image of the judicial function by acting very much like English judges. They were interpreting creatively, building a common law that was a rival to the law of the central government in Paris, and even developing their own doctrine of *stare decisis*.

With the revolution, and its consecration of the dogma of strict separation of powers, the judicial function was emphatically restricted. The revolutionary insistence that law be made only by a representative legislature meant that law could not be made, either directly or indirectly, by judges. One expression of this attitude was the requirement that the judge use only "the law" in deciding a case, and this meant, as we have seen in Chapter IV, that he could not base his decision on prior judicial decisions. The doctrine of *stare decisis* was rejected. Another expression of the dogma of strict separation of the legislative and judicial powers was the notion that judges should not interpret incomplete, conflicting, or unclear legislation. They should always refer such questions to the legislature for authoritative interpretation. It was expected that there would not be very many such situations, and that after a fairly brief period almost all the problems would be corrected and further resort to the legislature for interpretation would be unnecessary. (The history of the retreat from this position will be described in the next chapter.)

The picture of the judicial process that emerges is one of fairly routine activity. The judge becomes a kind of expert clerk. He is presented with a fact situation to which a ready legislative response will be readily found in all except the extraordinary case. His function is merely to find the right legislative provision, couple it with the fact situation, and bless the solution that is more or less automatically produced from the union. The whole process of judicial decision is made to fit into the formal syllogism of scholastic logic. The major premise is in the statute, the facts of the case furnish the minor premise, and

the conclusion inevitably follows. In the uncommon case in which some more sophisticated intellectual work is demanded of the judge, he is expected to follow carefully drawn directions about the limits of interpretation.

The net image is of the judge as an operator of a machine designed and built by legislators. His function is a mechanical one. The great names of the civil law are not those of judges (who knows the name of a civil law judge?) but those of legislators (Justinian, Napoleon) and scholars (Gaius, Irnerius, Bartolus, Mancini, Domat, Pothier, Savigny, and a host of other nineteenth- and twentieth-century European and Latin American scholars). The civil law judge is not a culture hero or a father figure, as he often is with us. His image is that of a civil servant who performs important but essentially uncreative functions.

It is a logical, if not a necessary, consequence of the quite different status of the civil law judge that he is not widely known, even among lawyers. His judicial opinions are not read in order to study his individual ways of thinking and his apparent preconceptions and biases. Although there are exceptions, the tendency is for the decisions of higher courts in civil law jurisdictions to be strongly collegial in nature. They are announced as the decision of the court, without enumeration of votes pro and con among the judges. In most jurisdictions separate concurring opinions and dissenting opinions are not written or published, nor are dissenting votes noted. The tendency is to think of the court as a faceless unit.

The result is that although there is a superficial similarity of function between the civil law judge and the common law judge, there are substantial disparities in their accepted roles. In part the contemporary civil law judge inherits a status and serves a set of functions determined by a tradition going back to the *iudex* of Roman times. This tradition, in which the judge has never been conceived of as playing a very creative part, was reinforced by the anti-judicial ideology of the European revolution and the logical consequences of a rationalistic doctrine of strict separation of powers. The civil law judge thus plays a substantially more modest role than the judge in the common law tradition, and the system of selection and tenure of civil law judges is consistent with this quite different status of the judicial profession.

The establishment of rigid constitutions and the institution of judicial review of the constitutionality of legislation in some civil law jurisdictions has to some extent modified the traditional image of the civil law judge. In some jurisdictions (e.g. Italy and Germany), special constitutional courts have been established. These special courts, which are not part of the ordinary judicial system and are not manned by members of the ordinary judiciary, were established in response to the civil law tradition that judges (i.e. *ordinary* judges—the modern successors of the Roman *iudex* and the civil judges of the jus commune) cannot be given such power. With the establishment of these special courts manned by specially selected judges, tradition is, at least in form, observed. Indeed, a few purists within the civil law tradition suggest that it is wrong to call such constitutional courts "courts" and their members "judges." Because judges cannot make law, the reasoning goes, and because the power to hold statutes illegal is a form of lawmaking, these officials obviously cannot be judges and these institutions cannot be courts. But even where, as in some nations in Latin America, the power of judicial review resides in ordinary courts, the traditional civil law image of the judge retains most of its power. Judicial service is a bureaucratic career; the judge is a functionary, a civil servant; the judicial function is narrow, mechanical, and uncreative.

# VII

# THE INTERPRETATION OF STATUTES

IT HAS BEEN shown in earlier chapters that the doctrine of separation of powers, when carried to an extreme, led to the conclusion that courts should be denied any interpretive function and should be required to refer problems of statutory interpretation to the legislature itself for solution. The legislature would then provide an authoritative interpretation to guide the judge. In this way defects in the law would be cured, courts would be prevented from making law, and the state would be safe from the threat of judicial tyranny. To the civil law fundamentalist, authoritative interpretation by the lawmaker was the only permissible kind of interpretation.

The nearest approach to that ideal to be found in the modern history of a major nation is the attempt of Frederick the Great to make the law of Prussia judge-proof, toward the end of the eighteenth century. Under Frederick, Prussia adopted a code containing over 16,000 articles (by comparison, the Code Napoléon contains 2,281 articles). The Prussian code was an attempt to provide a specific, detailed solution for specific, detailed fact situations; the end sought was a complete catalog of such solutions, available to the judge for any case that might come before him. At the same time, the judge was forbidden to interpret the code. In case of doubt, he was to refer the question to a special Statutes Commission created for that purpose. If he were caught interpreting, the judge would incur Frederick's "disfavor" and would be severely punished. German legal historians tell us that the Statutes Commission never played the role Frederick intended for it; that the code, detailed as it was, did not provide obvious answers for all cases; and that the judges perforce interpreted its provisions in their daily work. Frederick's code, his commission, and his prohibition of judicial interpretation are all considered failures.

The development of French *cassation* (from *casser*, meaning "to quash") is the next logical, as well as chronological, step. The defects

and inconveniences of total reliance on authoritative interpretation were apparent to practical men of law in revolutionary France. They knew that the legislature would find itself flooded with difficult, often seemingly trivial, requests for interpretation, and that it would find the work of responding to such requests tiresome. The legislature was faced, however, with a theoretical dilemma: it might wish to avoid having to decide a constant stream of questions from the courts, but it could not allow the courts themselves to do the interpreting without undermining the doctrine of the separation of powers.

The solution chosen was, under the circumstances, perfectly understandable. A new governmental organ was created by the legislature and given the power to quash incorrect interpretations by the courts. In the legislative debates and in the law eventually promulgated, it was made clear that the new organ was not a part of the judicial system, but rather a special instrument created by the legislature to protect legislative supremacy from judicial usurpation. Although it looked and acted very much like a court, the legislature preserved appearances by calling it the Tribunal of Cassation, and describing it as "auprès du corps legislatif." The requirements of the separation of powers were met; legislative supremacy was upheld. Ordinary judges were to be kept from interpreting the statutes, and the legislature did not have to do such work.

It will be noted that the Tribunal of Cassation was not itself expected to provide authoritative interpretations of the statutes involved in the cases that came before it. On the contrary, its original function, consistent with its separate, nonjudicial nature, was merely to quash judicial decisions based on incorrect interpretations of statutes. Such cases would then go back to the judiciary for reconsideration and decision; that was, after all, a *judicial* function. Unlike the typical action of an appellate court in the United States, which not only quashes the incorrect decision of a question of law by the lower court, but also indicates the proper answer to the legal question incorrectly decided below and applies that result to the case to produce a new decision, the French Tribunal of Cassation was created to perform only the first of these steps. However, by a gradual, but apparently inevitable, process of evolution, the tribunal came to perform the second step,

as well as the first. Thus it not only indicated that the judicial decision was wrong; it also explained what the correct interpretation of the statute was. During this same period, the tribunal's nonjudicial origin dropped from view, and it came to be called the Court of Cassation; thus judicialized, it assumed a position at the apex of the system of ordinary courts. In France, as well as in Italy and other nations that have followed the French model, the full title is likely to be Supreme Court of Cassation. Thus the highest civil and criminal court in the jurisdiction—one that is manned by judges and that has primary responsibility for assuring the correct and uniform interpretation and application of the statutes by the lower civil and criminal courts—is the direct descendant of a legislative tribunal originally created to keep the power of interpretation out of the hands of judges.

The final step in the evolution of such bodies is illustrated by the German institution of "revision," as distinguished from the French cassation. The French system stopped at the second step: the Supreme Court of Cassation could quash a decision based on an incorrect interpretation, and it could instruct the lower court as to the correct interpretation. Still, the case had to be sent back to the lower court for decision. This was often a mere formality that unnecessarily took up valuable time; and occasionally more serious problems arose because lower judges were either unable or unwilling to understand and follow the interpretation announced by the Supreme Court of Cassation. Much of the history of the process of cassation since the court's creation is the chronicle of such problems and of the various devices that have been invented to solve them. By the time Germany was united under Bismarck, the defects of French cassation were clearly apparent. And by that time European legal thought had openly conceded that judges did, indeed, have to interpret statutes as part of their ordinary work. There was no reason to complicate matters unnecessarily, so the Germans did the rational thing: they created a supreme court with the power to review the decisions of lower courts for legal correctness, to quash incorrect decisions, to indicate the correct answer, and to "revise" the incorrect decision accordingly.

The evolution from the argument for compulsory referral to the legislature for interpretation, through referral to a legislative tribunal,

to emergence of a court with the power to review and correct inter-pretations by lower courts has necessarily been accompanied by a gradual acceptance of a power of interpretation by the ordinary judi-ciary. This evolution has also been accompanied by an enormous amount of discussion and writing, some of it to justify interpretation of statutes by courts, some of it to define the limits of the interpretative power, and some of it to specify how that power should be exercised. The mass of scholarship on interpretation in civil law countries (which is roughly analogous to the mass of literature in the United States on the judicial process) thus is in part an expression of uneasiness over the fact that courts are interpreting statutes, in part an expression of anxiety that they will abuse their power of interpretation; only a small proportion of it focuses on the actual process of interpretation. Many writers have sought to prove that judicial interpretation is not really in conflict with legislative supremacy and a strict separation of powers. Those interested in defining the limits of interpretation have been concerned with certainty in the law and the prevention of judicial tyranny and irresponsibility. Only a few writers have tried to give the judge help in facing up to particular problems of interpretation.

As we have seen, revolutionary ideology assumed that systematic legislation would be clear, complete, and coherent, reducing the func-tion of the judge to one of merely applying the law (i.e. the statute) to the facts. This simplistic view of the judicial process, which has an amazing power of survival in the minds of laymen and some lawyers, is the precise equivalent of a simplistic attitude toward the work of judges in the common law world. Many laymen among us, and even some lawyers, persist in believing that courts are bound by prior deci-sions and that the process of finding and applying the precedent to the case is relatively mechanical. There is a folklore of the judicial process at work in both the common law and the civil law traditions.

Actually, it is extremely unlikely that thoughtful Continental jurists ever had much confidence in such a vision of the legal process. During the period of revolutions, it might have seemed important to act as though the revolutionary ideology were valid, but it is inconceivable that many legal scholars ever believed in it. It is too obvious that the facts are sharply different from the ideology. For one thing, the illu-

sion of the self-applying statute, the legislative norm so clear that its application is an automatic process, was long ago dispelled by exposure to the facts. Ever since the revolutionary period, civil law courts have been engaged in hearing and deciding disputes whose resolution depends on the meaning to be given to a legislative provision. Such litigation is frequently appealed, and reversals of lower court decisions are far from uncommon. Hardly an article in a typical civil code has escaped the need for judicial interpretation to supply a meaning that was unclear to the parties, to their counsel, or to the judges themselves.

Likewise the dogma that a code can be complete and coherent fails to survive even a cursory glance at the jurisprudence (the civil law term for judicial decisions). The books are full of decisions in which the court has had to fill gaps in the legislative scheme and reconcile apparently conflicting statutes. Although the text of a statute remains unchanged, its meaning and application often change in response to social pressures, and new problems arise that are not even touched on by any existing legislation. The ideal of certainty in the law becomes unattainable in the face of the uncertainty that exists in fact, where determination of the rights of parties frequently must await the results of litigation. The judge is not, in practice, relieved by clear, complete, coherent, prescient legislation from the necessity of interpreting and applying statutes. Like the common law judge, he is engaged in a vital, complex, and difficult process. He must apply statutes that are seldom, if ever, clear in the context of the case, however clear they may seem to be in the abstract. He must fill gaps and resolve conflicts in the legislative scheme. He must adapt the law to changing conditions. The code is not self-evident in application, particularly to the thoughtful judge.

Despite these facts, the folklore of judicial interpretation has had surprising persistence in the civil law world. As a result, there is a tension between fact and folklore, and a substantial literature attempting to resolve that tension has grown up. Until recently the principal effort in that literature has been to try to preserve the folklore by explaining away the facts. Typically that literature approaches the topic under three headings: (1) the problem of interpretation in the strict sense, i.e. the unclear provision; (2) the problem of lacunae, i.e.

44

the nonexistent provision; and (3) the problem of so-called evolutive interpretation, i.e. the statute whose meaning changes while its terms remain constant.

Each of these is a problem because of the requirement that the judge decide the case. He is not allowed to say that the law is unclear and therefore dismiss the action. The problem of interpretation in the strict sense then becomes one of justifying a decision by the judge when the legislative direction is unclear. This both makes the judge the lawmaker for the case and exposes the parties to the risk of judicial irresponsibility and arbitrariness. It is even worse in the case of lacunae, where the legislature has failed to provide any rule. Here the judge clearly is legislating for the case, and the dangers are even more apparent. And where, by judicial interpretation, a statute comes to mean something different from what it meant at the time it was enacted, the role of judge as lawmaker seems obvious.

The orthodox civil law response to the problems of interpretation is well illustrated in the provision of the Italian Civil Code of 1942 dealing with the interpretation of statutes:

In interpreting the statute, no other meaning can be attributed to it than that made clear by the actual significance of the words according to the connections between them, and by the intention of the legislature.

If a controversy cannot be decided by a precise provision, consideration is given to provisions that regulate similar cases or analogous matters; if the case still remains in doubt, it is decided according to general principles of the legal order of the State.

The first paragraph of this statute (which has itself been subject to a great deal of interpretation by Italian courts, producing a substantial body of interpretation about interpretation) is the legislative direction to the courts on the problem of interpretation in the strict sense. The statute should be applied according to its plain meaning and if that is unclear, the judge should look to the intention of the legislature in enacting the statute. Obviously, such directions to the judge say either too much or too little. If it is clear what is meant by the statute, then there is no problem. If it is not clear what is meant, "the actual significance of the words" is a mirage. Words have no inherent significance; they are supplied with meaning by those who use them, and the

problem before the judge is to supply meaning when it is not clear what the legislator meant when he used the words. The resort to legislative intent may be helpful in some cases, but reconstruction of the historical process of forming and expressing intent in a forum as complex as a representative legislature is a very risky enterprise. In a surprising number of cases, the legislative history will show that the legislature did not foresee the problem facing the judge, and consequently had no intent concerning it. Indeed, it is generally agreed among scholars that the search should be not for the actual legislative intent, but for the "intention, spirit, objective content of the norm [i.e. statute] itself." Such admonitions as those contained in the first paragraph of the Italian statute, and similar admonitions to judges in other civil law countries, consequently do not help the judge solve the problem of the unclear statute. They merely establish conceptual sets consistent with the orthodox view of judicial interpretation, and tell the judge that he must articulate his result in those terms. The judge is not told how to decide; he is to told how to state what he has decided.

The second paragraph of the statute is the direction to the judge regarding the problem of lacunae. If there is no statutory provision bearing precisely on the point, the judge is to reason by analogy from other statutory provisions. If this does not work, then he is to resort to something called "general principles of the legal order of the State," a provision that has emerged from many years of ideological debate. The analogous reference in the Austrian Civil Code of 1811 was to "the principles of natural law." That provision represented the general view prevailing before the ultimate victory of state positivism. The idea was that there was something called "natural law" existing apart from the positive law of any form of government and flowing from the nature of man and the natural requirements of order in society. During this period, the principal debate was between different schools of natural law and, in particular, between the secular and the Roman Catholic schools. Later in the nineteenth century the word "natural" was dropped from the usual formulations. This was clearly a step away from natural law and toward unchallenged state positivism, but it was not far enough away to still the debate. The formulation in the Italian statute quoted above has quieted all doubts in Italy. The ten-

dency in other civil law jurisdictions is also away from any reference to or reliance on natural law. As to the actual significance of the instructions concerning resolution of the problem of lacunae, we must wait until Chapter X and the discussion of legal science. There it will be shown that this sort of instruction to the judge is useful mainly as a means of reconciling the folklore of judicial interpretation with the dominant school of legal thought in the civil law world.

The most difficult problem of interpretation to solve in a manner consistent with legislative supremacy and the separation of powers is that of evolutive interpretation. The phenomenon is familiar enough: an old statute, if applied in the traditional way, will produce a clearly undesirable result in the case before the judge. It is not that the prior interpretation was wrong; often it will have been confirmed by a judgment of the Supreme Court of Cassation (or its equivalent). But circumstances may have changed sufficiently to require a different interpretation in the present case. The problem for the judge is that if he decides according to the old interpretation the result of the case will be offensive to him, to the parties, and to society. If he reinterprets the statute in order to achieve a result satisfactory to him, to the parties (at least one of them), and to society, he will be making law. He can, of course, defer to the legislature and refuse to reinterpret the statute, calling on the legislature to change the law to meet modern requirements. However, this would not give much satisfaction to the parties in the case, and it would make impossible demands on the legislature. Consequently there is general agreement in civil law jurisdictions that judges do have the power to interpret evolutively. The discussion thus shifts from the legitimacy of this function to the question of its justification and its proper limits. Predictably, the traditional scholarship on this problem of interpretation is concerned primarily with proving that the judge, in interpreting evolutively, does not really make law.

Much of the writing on the topic of judicial interpretation in the civil law world is, as has been suggested above, designed to prove the continuing validity of the folklore of judicial interpretation, and this view is still taught to law students by many professors. More recently, there have been a variety of reactions against the folklore. Such schools of thought as the jurisprudence of interests, sociological jurisprudence,

and legal realism, among others, have their partisans. In Switzerland, the civil code instructs the judge that when all aids to interpretation fail, he should employ the rule he would adopt if he were a legislator. In these and many other ways, the folklore of judicial interpretation is losing ground. Nonetheless, many still believe in it, and those who do not cannot ignore it; they must refute it. The folklore of judicial interpretation is a characteristic part of the civil law tradition.

As noted earlier, judicial decisions are not a source of law. It would violate the rules against judicial lawmaking if decisions of courts were to be binding on subsequent courts. The orthodox view consequently is that no court is bound by the decision of any other court in a civil law jurisdiction. In theory, at least, even though the highest court has already spoken on the question and indicated a clear view of its proper resolution, the lowest court in the jurisdiction can decide differently.

This is the theory, but the facts are different. Although there is no formal rule of *stare decisis*, the practice is for judges to be influenced by prior decisions. Judicial decisions are regularly published in most civil law jurisdictions. A lawyer preparing a case searches for cases in point and uses them in his argument; and the judge deciding a case often refers to prior cases. Whatever the ideology of the revolution may say about the value of precedent, the fact is that courts do not act very differently toward reported decisions in civil law jurisdictions than do courts in the United States. The judge may refer to a precedent because he is impressed by the authority of the prior court, because he is persuaded by its reasoning, because he is too lazy to think the problem through himself, because he does not want to risk reversal on appeal, or for a variety of other reasons. These are the principal reasons for the use of authority in the common law tradition, and the absence of any formal rule of *stare decisis* is relatively unimportant. Those who contrast the civil law and the common law traditions by a supposed nonuse of judicial authority in the former and a binding doctrine of precedent in the latter exaggerate on both sides. Everybody knows that civil law courts do use precedents. Everybody knows that common law courts distinguish cases they do not want to follow, and sometimes overrule their own decisions.

Even though these facts are obvious and widely known, the folklore

persists. Otherwise thoughtful civil lawyers frequently ignore the widespread use of precedent by their own courts, just as equally thoughtful common lawyers frequently oversimplify and misrepresent the use of precedent by common law courts. The important distinction between the civil law and the common law judicial processes does not lie in what courts in fact do, but in what the dominant folklore tells them they do. In the orthodox civil law tradition, the judge is assigned a comparatively minor, inglorious role as a mere operator of a machine designed and built by scholars and legislators. We now turn to an examination of the way this judicial image is reflected in the peculiar emphasis on certainty in the civil law and in the denial of inherent equitable power to civil law judges.

# VIII

## CERTAINTY AND EQUITY

THERE IS a great emphasis in the literature of the civil law tradition on the importance of certainty in the law. Certainty is, of course, an objective in all legal systems, but in the civil law tradition it has come to be a kind of supreme value, an unquestioned dogma, a fundamental goal. Even though most civil lawyers would recognize that there are competing values whose preservation might require some sacrifice of certainty, the matter is usually not discussed in these terms. In the civil law world it is always a good argument against a proposed change in the legal process that it will impair the certainty of the law. In Italy under Mussolini, for example, some attempts of the Fascists to make the law into an instrument of the totalitarian state were successfully resisted by jurists in the name of certainty in the law. After the fall of Fascism and the establishment of the republic, many desirable reforms in the Italian legal system were resisted by other jurists, again in the interests of certainty. It is an abstract legal value. Like a queen in chess, it can move in any direction.

Although the ideal of certainty has been used for a variety of purposes, its most important application is a reflection of the distrust of judges. Judges are prohibited from making law in the interest of certainty. Legislation should be clear, complete, and coherent in the interest of certainty. The process of interpretation and application of the law should be as automatic as possible, again in the interest of certainty. In this sense the emphasis on certainty is an expression of a desire to make the law judge-proof.

Legal certainty is also recognized as desirable in the common law tradition, but there are three major differences. First, certainty is usually discussed in more functional terms, and is not elevated to the level of dogma. It is recognized that people should, to the extent possible, know the nature of their rights and obligations and be able

to plan their actions with some confidence about the legal consequences; but it is also recognized that there are limits on the extent
to which certainty is possible. Second, certainty is achieved in the common law by giving the force of law to judicial decisions, something
theoretically forbidden in civil law. The accumulation of judicial decisions in the course of time in a jurisdiction provides a variety of concrete, detailed examples of legal rules in operation. These, together
with the statements of the rules themselves, are likely to provide more
certainty about the law than are broad legislative statements of the
rules. Thus, the desire for certainty is an argument in favor of *stare
decisis* in the common law tradition, whereas it is an argument against
*stare decisis* in the civil law tradition. Finally, in the common law
world (particularly in the United States) it is more generally recognized that certainty is only one of a number of legal values, which
sometimes conflict with each other. Certainty frequently implies rigidity; law that is certain may be difficult to mold in response to changed
circumstances or to bend to the requirements of a particular case. In
the common law, certainty and flexibility are seen as competing values,
each tending to limit the other. In the civil law world, the supreme
value is certainty, and the need for flexibility is seen as a series of
"problems" complicating progress toward the ideal of a judge-proof
law. Hence the concern described in the preceding chapter about interpretation by judges is frequently put in these terms: if judges are
not carefully controlled in the way they interpret legislation, the law
will be rendered more uncertain.

The same general attitude exists toward equity. In its general sense,
equity refers to the power of the judge to mitigate the harshness of
strict application of a statute, or to allocate property or responsibility
according to the facts of the individual case. Equity is, in other words,
a limited grant of power to the court to apply principles of fairness in
resolving a dispute being tried before it. It is a recognition that broad
rules, such as those commonly encountered in statutes, occasionally
work harshly or inadequately, and that some problems are so complex
that it is not possible for the legislature to dictate the consequences of
all possible permutations of the facts. Where problems like these are

involved, it is thought better to leave the matter to the trier of the case for decision according to equitable principles. Equity thus is the justice of the individual case. It clearly implies a grant of discretionary power to the judge.

But in the civil law tradition, to give discretionary power to the judge threatens the certainty of the law. As a matter of legal theory, the position has been taken that judges have no *inherent* equitable power. They may from time to time be granted authority to use equity in the disposition of a case, but this grant of power will be expressly made and carefully circumscribed in a statute enacted by the legislature. Although the matter has produced much discussion in the past, and is still the source of argument among civil law scholars, the dominant view is still that, in the interest of certainty, judges must be carefully restricted in the exercise of equity.

The civil law has, then, sacrificed flexibility for certainty. In contrast, the common law tends to strike the balance between them more equally. Some of the reasons for this difference in attitudes toward judicial discretion in the two legal traditions have already been described in the preceding two chapters. There is, however, an additional cause: the existence in England for several centuries of a separate system of chancery courts and a separate body of legal principles called equity.

The Norman conquerors of England at the Battle of Hastings quickly set about centralizing the government, including the administration of justice. They established royal courts and a system of royal justice that gradually displaced the old feudal courts and rules. In the process of centralizing English justice, the judges of the royal courts developed new procedures and remedies and a new body of substantive law, applicable, at least in theory, to all Englishmen. For this reason it was called the common law. The common law, at first dynamic and creative, eventually developed into a rigid, circumscribed set of procedures and remedies applied according to inflexible, technical rules. The common law became formula- and rule-bound. However, an individual who was dissatisfied with the remedy available to him in the royal courts, or who wished to complain about the fairness of a decision, could always petition the king for relief. The king had the

power to vary the operation of his system of justice on the basis of such petitions (a power that has a vestigial equivalent today in the power of a chief executive to pardon and commute).

From time to time the king himself may have considered and acted on such petitions, but before long the task was delegated to a royal official, called the chancellor. This official (often called "the king's conscience") was given the power to vary the operation of the law in the interests of fairness. There were, of course, many complaints about actual or fancied abuses of this discretionary power and about the uncertainty it involved; and at one time there was a popular saying to the effect that justice was measured by the length of the chancellor's foot. But as the process of hearing and acting on petitions for relief from the law became more institutionalized and formalized, and as the volume of business became sufficiently great to require assistants to help the chancellor decide, the discretionary grant of relief from the operation of the law became more and more judicialized. Formalities, rules of procedure, and substantive rules were developed to govern the submission of petitions to the chancellor and his action on them. By gradual degrees the chancellor became a court of chancery, and the rules applied in chancery proceedings became a separate body of law, called equity in recognition of the court of chancery's historical origins.

So for several centuries two separate systems of justice existed in England: the law courts and the common law on one side, and the chancery courts and equity on the other. In general, during their separate existence the jurisdiction of the chancery court was limited to ameliorating the harsh operation of some aspects of the common law and supplying remedies in cases where the common law remedy was considered inadequate. Eventually the separate systems of courts and of law and equity were abolished, and the jurisdictions and principles merged. The surviving common law tradition consequently consists of both the original common law and the tempering influence of equity.

A comparative law scholar has remarked that the civil law today is what the common law would look like if there had never been a court of chancery in England. There is some historical basis for such

a statement, since there has been nothing like the loosening and lib-eralizing influence of the court of chancery in the civil law tradition since early in the Roman period. More concretely, however, two spe-cific contributions of equity to the common law tradition help to explain the differences between the contemporary common law and civil law traditions. These are judicial discretion and the civil con-tempt power.

As to judicial discretion, common law judges traditionally have inherent equitable powers: they can mold the result in the case to the requirements of the facts, bend the rule where necessary to achieve substantial justice, and interpret and reinterpret in order to make the law respond to social change. These powers are not seen as threats to certainty in law; indeed certainty is to be achieved through the doc-trine of *stare decisis*, itself a judicial doctrine. The difficulties of ra-tionalizing the demand for certainty and the justice of the individual case thus become problems for solution by the judges themselves. There is no conflict on this question between the judicial and the legislative powers of government. In the common law the judge can exercise discretion, but he also must bear the major operational re-sponsibility for certainty and stability in the law.

Hence the common law judge is less compelled by prevailing at-titudes to cram the dispute into a box built by the legislature than is his civil law counterpart. Even when the case involves application of a statute, the common law judge has some measure of power to adjust the rule to the facts. If the box supplied by the legislature does not fit, the judge can make minor adjustments in it to make it fit. Where the applicable law is precedent, a box built by one or more prior judges, this power is even greater. In the civil law world, on the con-trary, if the facts do not fit the box, they must be forced out of shape in order to make them fit. And the box is, in theory, always built by the legislature.

It is one thing to say that the civil law judge lacks inherent equitable power. That statement is true insofar as it is the prevailing theory. It is quite another matter to accuse the civil law of being less equitable than the common law. That statement is demonstrably false. Indeed, a good argument can be (and has been) made that the civil law has

developed a better, because more equitable, body of substantive rules in some fields of law than has the Anglo-American system. Our concern here is not with relative fairness, but with the distribution of power between legislature and court. In the common law the judge has inherent equitable power. In the civil law tradition that power is in the legislature. The way in which the legislature exercises that power, and the resulting effect on the judiciary, provides an excellent example of the contrast between the theory and the practice of the legal process in the civil law tradition.

The theory is that the legislature exercises its equitable power in either of two principal ways: it can specifically delegate that power, in carefully defined situations, to the judge, or it can itself enact rules of equity for the judge to apply like other rules. An example of the first type is found in Article 1226 of the Italian civil code, which tells the judge that if the precise amount of the damage to the plaintiff resulting from a breach of the defendant's obligation cannot be proved, the judge shall fix the amount according to equitable principles. An example of the second type is found in Article 1337 of the same code, which provides that the parties to a contract shall act in good faith in the negotiation and formation of the contract. Any modern civil code anywhere in the civil law world will contain a number of such provisions.

It requires no great exercise of imagination to realize that the second type of statute in effect transfers a large segment of undefined equitable power to the judge. It is true that the legislature has acted and that its action is expressed as a substantive rule of law, but the terms are so broad ("good faith," which is not defined in the code, has an almost unlimited area of potential application) that the judge is hardly constrained by the legislative formulation. What that statute means depends on what judges do with it in concrete cases. What they do with it in concrete cases becomes the law in fact, although not in theory. A lawyer who wants to learn what effect to anticipate from the application of that statute will turn immediately to reported decisions in which it has been applied by courts. The legislature has not provided the box; it has, in effect, told the judges to make the box themselves.

55

The practice of delegating power to courts through legislation that employs general clauses of this sort is a common one in the civil law world, although the extent to which judges have consciously exercised that power varies widely. Article 1382 of the Code Napoléon provides that one whose act injures another must compensate him for the injury. The French courts have built an entire body of tort law on the basis of that article. Article 242 of the German *bürgerliches Gesetzbuch* (BGB) requires a person to perform his obligation in the manner required by good faith. The German courts have employed this statute to create an immense body of new law on the performance of obligation. Both sets of courts have, in the process, developed working attitudes toward case law that are much more like those of common law courts than the prevailing theory admits. The German courts have been particularly overt about it, and their reliance on Article 242 to deal with some of the problems arising out of Germany's disastrous post–World War I inflation provides an example of judicial activism that seems extreme even to hardened legal realists.

At the same time, the compliance of German judges with the wishes of the Nazi regime is often unfavorably compared with the more successful resistance of Italian judges to the Fascists. The German judges, so the argument goes, had aggressively opted for judicial discretion at the expense of certainty in the 1920's, both to justify their use of general clauses and to follow the theory advanced by the "free law" school of jurists. The Italian judges stayed with their traditional approach of emphasizing certainty and exercising only a very limited degree of discretion. When darkness fell, the German judges were unable to defend the legal order by calling on the importance of certainty. Unlike the Italians, they had openly abandoned that principle. Whether one is persuaded by this version of history or not is unimportant. The fact that many do believe it gives us some insight into the continuing vitality of the appeal to certainty and the continuing distrust of judicial discretion that one finds in even the most liberated of civil law nations.

A second major distinguishing contribution of equity to the common law tradition is the civil contempt power. This is the power of

a court in a civil (i.e. noncriminal) case to punish a person who violates a court order to perform or to refrain from performing an act. The idea is that the court can order a person to do something or not to do something and punish him if he disobeys the order. The contempt power is used for a wide variety of purposes in the common law. Someone living near an airport who is annoyed by airplanes flying too low over his property may get an injunction against further flights below a certain altitude. If the injunction is disobeyed, the offender can be punished by the court. One who has promised to convey some land to another and who subsequently refuses to do so may be ordered to do so by the court, and if he refuses, can be punished for his refusal. A labor group illegally picketing an employer can be enjoined from continuing to picket, and the responsible officials of the union can be punished if the picketing does not stop. The variety of situations in which such orders addressed to individuals are employed as a remedy in the common law is very great. The power behind these orders is the power of the court to punish individuals for failing to obey them—the contempt power.

There is no civil contempt power in the civil law tradition. A general power to address orders to specific persons and to punish them for failure to follow the orders is unknown. The French do have something they call the *astreinte*, which appears, in a limited way, to be a functional equivalent of the contempt power; and something like the *astreinte* can also be found in German law. But these are pale imitations of the broad power of the common law judge.

The very idea of giving a court the general power to compel individuals in civil actions to do or to refrain from doing certain acts under penalty of imprisonment or fine or both is repugnant to the civil law tradition. For one thing, it is inconsistent with the demand for certainty; it gives the judge a great deal more power than civil lawyers think judges ought to have. In addition, fines and imprisonment for refusal to obey orders sound to civil law jurists more like criminal than civil penalties. Accordingly, the view is that the substantive and procedural safeguards incorporated in criminal law and criminal procedure are usually necessary before the imposition of penalties on individuals. Such safeguards do not exist within the non-

criminal law. Finally, the civil contempt power does not seem necessary to the administration of justice in the civil law tradition. The assumption is that the individual's property will answer for his obligations. The power of the civil court is usually limited to the giving of money judgments, based on express statutory authorization, in all but one class of cases. In the exceptional situation, the civil court may order the doing of an act, but only where the act is one than can be performed by a third person—a so-called "fungible act." The cost of the performance can then be charged to the defendant and, if necessary, the appropriate legal significance can be given to the act by the judge. For example, where one who has the legal obligation to do so does not execute the instrument needed to convey land, the court may have the appropriate instrument prepared, and may give it the necessary legal effect.

The different kind of emphasis on certainty, and the presence or absence of inherent judicial discretion and the contempt power, thus exemplify the fundamental differences in the roles of the judiciary in the two legal traditions. They reveal the extent to which the civil law judge is still limited by a variety of historical influences, most prominently by the image of the judicial process that emerged in the period of the French Revolution and by the refinement of that image that took place under the impact of legal science, to which we now turn.

# IX

## SCHOLARS

W<small>E HAVE</small> seen that the role of the civil law judge is generally thought to be much more restricted and modest than that of the common law judge. It is reasonable to speak of the common law as a law of the judges, but no one would think of using such terms in speaking of the civil law. The image of the Roman *iudex*, the alleged abuses perpetrated by judges under the old regime, and the conception of the role of judges that emerged in France during the revolution converge to limit what judges are supposed to do. Legislative positivism, the dogma of the separation of powers, the ideology of codification, the attitude toward interpretation of statutes, the peculiar emphasis on certainty, the denial of inherent equitable power in the judge, and the rejection of the doctrine of *stare decisis*—all these tend to diminish the judge and to glorify the legislator.

From this, one might suppose that the protagonist of the legal process in the civil law tradition is the legislator. It was hoped for a time that the legislature would produce bodies of law that were complete, coherent, and clear, so that interpretation would be unnecessary. The retreat from the dogma of legislative infallibility has been a slow, grudging one. Although it is now admitted that civil law courts have an interpretive function, the fiction is still maintained that in performing that function the judge does not create law, but merely seeks and follows the expressed or implied intent of the legislator. All this suggests that the civil law legislator occupies the dominant position held in the common law tradition by the judge. For brief periods in the history of the civil law tradition this may have been true, but the legislators soon found themselves again in the shadow of the men who were primarily responsible for the theory of the modern nation-state, for the doctrines of legislative positivism and the separation of powers, for the form, style and content of codification, and for the dominant view of the nature of the judicial function. The teacher-scholar is the

real protagonist of the civil law tradition. The civil law is a law of the professors.

By way of contrast, although the influence of law professors and legal scholarship may be growing in the United States, judges still exercise the most important influence in shaping the growth and development of the American legal system. Moreover, the prevailing ideology assumes that they play this role, and they themselves are conscious of what is expected of them. The tradition of the scholar as an important force in the development of the common law is very recent and still, comparatively, very weak. The common law is still a law of the judges.

The preeminence of the scholar in the civil law tradition is very old. The Roman jurisconsult—who advised the praetor and the judge, was recognized as an expert on the law, but had no legislative or judicial responsibility—is considered to be the founder of this scholarly tradition. His opinions had great weight, and during the second century A.D. the opinions of certain jurisconsults were binding on judges. Their opinions were written down, collected, and treated as authoritative. Much of the most important part of Justinian's *Corpus Juris Civilis*— parts of the *Digest* and all of the *Institutes*—is made up of the work of jurisconsults.

After the revival of Roman law in Italy, those responsible for the revival and development of the medieval jus commune were scholars. The work of the Glossators and the Commentators, added to Justinian's *Corpus Juris Civilis*, made up the body of Roman law received throughout Western Europe. During this period the responses of scholars to questions of law were in some places given binding authority in courts, a practice analogous to the use made of jurisconsults during the classical period of Roman law. Many of the codes drafted in Europe and in Latin America during the nineteenth century were the work of scholars, and all were based on the writings of earlier generations of scholars. The great debate about codification in Germany was begun and conducted by scholars. In Italy, which is in many ways the archetypal civil law jurisdiction, three recent prime ministers and one president have been law professor–scholars.

It is instructive to reexamine the role of scholars in the two great

legislative periods in the history of the civil law tradition—that of Justinian and that of codification in the nineteenth century. It will be recalled that Justinian was much concerned with the work of scholars. The accumulated mass of writing about the law was, in his view, a source of unnecessary confusion and difficulty. He did not, however, propose to abolish the authority of all the jurisconsults. Instead, he wished to select from the existing mass of legal scholarship whatever was worthy of preservation. This was one of the assignments he gave to the commission appointed to compile the *Corpus Juris Civilis*, a commission composed entirely of scholars. The *Digest*, which is the largest and most important part of the *Corpus Juris Civilis*, is in large part a compilation of the work of Roman legal scholars. The *Institutes*, another part of the *Corpus Juris Civilis*, is basically a textbook on Roman law written by scholars of the classical period.

The French codification movement also relied heavily on the work of scholars, although Napoleon himself took an active part in its preparation and enactment. The actual work of drafting the French codes was put into the hands of commissions composed of lawyers and judges; but these commissions were dominated by the work of scholars (particularly that of Robert Pothier), and the changes made in their drafts by the legislature were merely minor variations within the commissioners' grand scholarly design. A large part of the ideology of French codification came from scholarly and philosophical sources, including the works of men like Montesquieu and Rousseau. This ideology later dominated the interpretation and application of the codes in France, and was adopted in civil law nations that drafted their codes on the lines of the French model, again under the influence of men of learning (e.g. the Latin American Andrès Bello). The German codification, as we shall see, was even more thoroughly dominated by scholars.

Why, then, the curious ambivalence of the legislator toward the scholar? Why, for example, did Justinian forbid the preparation of commentaries on the *Corpus Juris Civilis*? One can only guess. His desire to restore the classical Roman law of an earlier, greater period may have been accompanied by the fear that commentaries prepared

during his lifetime or at some subsequent time would be of a lower quality. Like much of the work excluded from the *Corpus Juris Civilis,* they would be inferior to the scholarship of the classical period. A second possibility is that Justinian thought that his compilation represented perfection, so that any commentary could only detract from its merit. Third, as Emperor of the Roman Empire, Justinian saw the *Corpus Juris Civilis,* officially promulgated by him, as the reigning body of law for the empire, and believed that commentaries on his legislation might tend to impair its authority. Justinian's prohibition against the publication of commentaries was, of course, ignored during his lifetime.

Although he did not attempt to forbid them, Napoleon hoped that no commentaries on his civil code would be published. This hope, like Justinian's command, was ineffectual. According to a well-worn story, his reaction when he was informed that the first commentary had been published was to exclaim: "My code is lost." One reason for such a statement was the illusion that the code was so clear, complete, and coherent that commentaries on it were superfluous. Another was the fear that once the code fell into the hands of legal scholars, its usefulness as a popular law book for the French citizen would be diminished. Another may have been apprehension about the tendency of scholars to think in conservative, historical terms. Napoleon wanted his code to transcend the old regional divisions and to provide the basis for a completely new legal order. All prior law on topics covered by the code was repealed, but the new law had to be protected against interpretation according to prerevolutionary legal ideas in order to make that repeal effective. Scholars were unlikely to agree with the patriotic lawyer who was quoted as saying: "I know nothing of the civil law; I know only the Code Napoléon."

Thus both Justinian and Napoleon called on prominent jurists to carry out the very complicated task of drafting far-reaching legal reforms. But they feared the influence of scholars on their reforms. Other evidences of legislative distrust of legal scholarship frequently crop up in the civil law world. In contemporary Italy, for example, the legislature has told the courts that they may not cite books and articles in their opinions. Therefore Italian judges, who are heavily

influenced by legal scholarship, employ the ideas suggested to them by scholars without citing them, and refer in a very general way to "the doctrine," which is the civil law term for books and articles written by legal scholars. This easy circumvention of the Italian parliament's command is merely another example of the futility of legislative attempts to eliminate or even reduce the influence of the scholar in the civil law world. Despite legislative efforts to dam it, the great stream of legal scholarship in the civil law tradition moves on, providing the ideology and the basic content of legislation and eventually engulfing it.

We begin to understand the true importance of the civil law scholar when we look at a typical book on Continental legal history. Much of what is called legal history in the civil law tradition is baffling to the common lawyer who first approaches it. He is used to thinking of legal history as an account of legal rules and institutions in their historical, economic, and social contexts. The legal history he reads is full of great cases, occasional statutes, and historical events. But when he picks up a book on legal history in the civil law tradition, he is likely to find the bulk of it devoted to a discussion of schools of legal thought and of disputes between legal scholars and their followers. He will read about the Glossators, the Commentators, the Humanists, about the differences among the French scholars of the eighteenth century, and about the debate between Savigny and Anton Thibaut on codification in Germany. All in all, it is a peculiar form of intellectual history, almost entirely divorced from socioeconomic history on the one hand, and from discussion of the origin and development of specific legal institutions on the other. The protagonist of this form of legal history is the legal scholar, and its subject matter is currents of thought about the structure and operation of the legal order.

This is what we mean when we say that the legal scholar is the great man of the civil law. Legislators, executives, administrators, judges, and lawyers all come under his influence. He molds the civil law tradition and the formal materials of the law into a model of the legal system. He teaches this model to law students, and writes about it in books and articles. Legislators and judges accept his idea of what law is, and, when they make or apply law, they use concepts he has de-

veloped. Thus although legal scholarship is not a formal source of law, the doctrine carries immense authority.

In the United States, where the legislature is also theoretically supreme, there is a well-known saying (originated by a judge) that the law is what the judges say it is. This is, properly understood, a realistic statement of fact. The judge has to decide how to characterize a legal problem presented to him, which principles of law to apply to the problem, and how to apply them in order to arrive at a result. Whether the principles he chooses are embodied in legislation or in prior decisions, they achieve substantive meaning only in the context of a specific problem, and the meaning attributed to them in that context is necessarily the meaning supplied by the judge. In a similar sense it is reasonably accurate to say that the law in a civil law jurisdiction is what the scholars say it is. We now turn to a description of the concept of the law that has been developed and is being perpetuated by scholars in civil law countries.

# X

# LEGAL SCIENCE

IN CIVIL law jurisdictions, the way legal scholars look at the law is the way everyone looks at it. This was true in Bologna after the revival of Roman legal studies, where the dominant point of view about what law was and how it should be studied and taught was developed by the men called Glossators. When one refers to the work of the Glossators, one refers to their objectives, their methods, and their image of the legal process, as well as to their views on specific legal problems.

As the influence of the Glossators waned, a new group of scholars, the Commentators, gained ascendancy. The view of the law held by the Commentators, and their method of studying and teaching law, came to be called the Italian style (*mos italicus*). The Commentators and the Italian style were succeeded by the Humanists and the French style (*mos gallicus*), and later other schools arose. At any given moment in the history of the civil law tradition a number of different points of view will be in competition with each other, but one or another will always tend to dominate. The contemporary civil law world is still under the sway of one of the most powerful and coherent schools of thought in the history of the civil law tradition. We will call it legal science. It is the fifth component of the civil law tradition (after Roman civil law, canon law, commercial law, and the legacy of the revolutionary period) and the final one to be discussed in this book.

Legal science is primarily the creation of German legal scholars of the middle and late nineteenth century, and it evolved naturally out of the ideas of Savigny. As explained in Chapter IV, Savigny argued that German codification should not follow the rationalist and secular natural law thinking that characterized the French codification. He maintained that a satisfactory legal system had to be based on the principles of law that had historically been in force in Germany.

Therefore a necessary preliminary step to codification was a thorough historical study of the legal order to identify and properly state these principles and to arrange them in a coherent system.

Because private law, and particularly that part of it we have called Roman civil law, was thought to be the heart of the legal system, the German scholars put their principal efforts into thorough historical study and restatement of the principles of Roman civil law as received in Germany and as modified by the addition of Germanic elements. They concentrated their study on the *Digest* (in German, *Pandekten*, from the Latin *Pandectae*) of Justinian, and thus came to be called the Pandectists. They produced highly systematic treatises based on principles they discovered in their study of the Roman law. The *Digest* had been studied systematically for centuries, but the mid-nineteenth-century Germans brought this study to its highest and most systematic level. Their work culminated in the publication of influential treatises and, impelled by the unification of Germany under Bismarck in 1871, in the promulgation of the German Civil Code of 1896 (the BGB). The treatises and the BGB were influential throughout the civil law world (and also, to some extent, in the common law world, where there was a flurry of enthusiasm for legal science). The methods and the concepts developed by the German scholars were applied to other fields of law, both private and public, and hence came to dominate legal scholarship. Despite a variety of criticisms and reactions against it from the time of Savigny to the present, legal science continues to affect the thinking of civil law scholars, and hence of other men of law, in the civil law tradition.

The concept of legal science rests on the assumption that the materials of the law (statutes, regulations, customary rules, etc.) are naturally occurring phenomena, or data from the study of which the legal scientist can discover certain principles and relationships, just as the physical scientist discovers natural laws from the study of physical data. As a leading German scholar of the time, Rudolph Sohm, put it: "The scientific process, by means of which principles are discovered that are not immediately contained in the sources of law, may be compared to the analytical methods of chemistry." Under the influence

of this kind of thinking, legal scholars deliberately and conscientiously sought to emulate natural scientists. They thought they were employing the scientific method, and they sought admission to the community of scientists. (It should be added that similar assumptions, but with less emphasis on science and the scientific method, underlay some of the work of legal scholars in the United States in the late nineteenth century, and still constitute one source of justification for the famous case method of teaching in American law schools.)

Legal science is also highly systematic. Principles derived from a scientific study of legal data are made to fit together in a very intricate way. As new principles are discovered they must be fully integrated into the system. If new data do not fit, either the system must be modified to accommodate them, or they must be modified to fit the system. In this way the preservation of systematic values becomes an important consideration in criticizing and reforming the law.

This emphasis on systematic values tends to produce a great deal of interest in definitions and classifications. Much scholarly effort has gone into the development and refinement of definitions of concepts and classes, which are then taught in a fairly mechanical, uncritical way. The assumption of legal science that it scientifically derives concepts and classes from the study of natural legal data on the one hand, and the generally authoritarian and uncritical nature of the process of legal education on the other, tend to produce the attitude that definitions of concepts and classes express scientific truth. A definition is not seen as something conventional, valid only so long as it is useful; it becomes a truth, the embodiment of reality. Serious arguments are conducted by grown men about the "autonomy" of certain fields of law, such as commercial law or agrarian law, or about the "true" nature of specific legal institutions. Law is divided up into clearly delimited fields. Public law and private law, as will be explained more fully in the next chapter, are treated as inherently different and clearly distinguishable. There is a precisely defined legal vocabulary, and an accepted classification of law that is reflected in the curricula of the law schools, in the professorial chairs in the faculties of law, in the arrangement of books in law libraries, in the

subject matter of works written by legal scholars, and in the approach of legislators to lawmaking.

The order thus imposed on the legal system by legal science represents a great systematic achievement. Civil lawyers are justly proud of their legal structure and methodology and of the very real contribution it makes to the certain, orderly, and efficient statement, elaboration, and administration of the law. Every phase of the legal process is a beneficiary of this systematic jurisprudence, and the absence of anything equivalent to it in the common law is one of the reasons why civil lawyers think of the common law as crude and undeveloped.

Because the components of this systematic restatement of the law, although theoretically inherent in the existing positive legal order, did not exist there in identified, articulated form, and because the legal order was a universe of data within which inherent principles were to be identified, new concepts had to be invented to express these components and principles. The novelty of these concepts and their prominence in the work of scholars committed to legal science eventually led critics to call this kind of doctrine "conceptual jurisprudence." Since communication without concepts is difficult, it hardly seems fair to criticize legal science for using them. What was peculiar to legal science was that its concepts were new (or were given a new emphasis), that the accent was on their "validity" rather than their functional utility, that their proper arrangement and manipulation were thought to be the province of scholars, and that they tended to be highly abstract.

This high level of abstraction—this tendency to make the facts recede—is one of the most striking characteristics of legal science to a lawyer from the United States or England. The principles developed by legal scientists have been taken out of their factual and historical context, and are consequently lacking in concreteness. The legal scientist is more interested in developing and elaborating a theoretical scientific structure than he is in solving concrete problems. He is in quest of the ever more pervasive legal truth, and in the process of making statements more abstract, "accidental" details are dropped. The ultimate objective is a general theory of law from which all but the essential elements have been removed.

The work of legal science is carried on according to the methods of traditional formal logic. The scholar takes the raw materials of the law and, by a process called "logical expansion," reasons to higher levels and broader principles. These principles themselves reveal on further study the even broader principles of which they are only specific representations, and so on up the scale. The principles derived by logical expansion are, at one level, the "provisions that regulate similar cases or analogous matters" and, at a higher level, the "general principles of the legal order of the state" that judges should employ in interpreting statutes (see Chapter VII). Intuition and the subconscious, despite their powerful influence on human affairs, are excluded from this process. The result is a kind of formalistic rationalism.

Finally, legal science attempts to be pure. Legal scientists deliberately focus their attention on pure legal phenomena and values, such as the "legal" value of certainty in the law, and exclude all others. Hence the data, insights, and theories of the social sciences, for example, are excluded as nonlegal. Even history is excluded as nonlegal—and this seems peculiarly inconsistent in view of the fact that Savigny and his disciples are called the historical school. It is of interest to historians (including legal historians) but not to legal science. Nor is the legal scientist interested in the ends of law, in such ultimate values as justice. These may properly be the concern of philosophers, including legal philosophers, but the legal scientist is concerned only with the law and with purely legal values. The result is a highly artificial body of doctrine that is deliberately insulated from what is going on outside, in the rest of the culture.

However, although legal scientists sought to be value-free and pure, they were ideological captives of their era. The creative work of the legal scientists took place in nineteenth-century Europe, in the intellectual climate that has since come to be called nineteenth-century European liberalism. Among the more relevant aspects of this ideology was a strong emphasis on the individual and his autonomy. Private property and liberty of contract were treated as fundamental institutions that should be limited as little as possible. It was an era of what we would now consider exaggerated individualism. The heart of the law was the Roman civil law, and the Roman civil law was basically

a law of property and contract. Legal scientists concentrated their work in this area of civil law, and the body of doctrine they eventually produced embodied the assumptions and values central to the thought of their time. Under the banner of legal science they built ideologically loaded concepts into a systematic conceptual legal structure that is still taught in the faculties of law of the universities, that limits and directs the thinking of the legal scholars who perpetuate it, that provides the parameters of judicial interpretation and application of laws, precedents, and legal transactions, and that, in a word, dominates the legal process. The role of these assumptions and values is concealed behind a façade of ideological neutrality, of the scientific study of purely legal phenomena. In this way European systematic jurisprudence embodies and perpetuates nineteenth-century liberalism, locking in a selected set of assumptions and values and locking out all others.

The special attitudes and assumptions about law that characterized the work of the Pandectists and that make up what is here called legal science can thus be summarized in the following terms: scientism, system-building, conceptualism, abstraction, formalism, and purism. These characteristics of legal science are apparent to many civil lawyers, and there have been many reactions against it in the civil law world. These reactions have taken a variety of forms, and they seem to have been gathering force in the period since World War II; but legal science is far from dead. In all except the most advanced civil law jurisdiction it reigns practically undisturbed. It dominates the faculties of law, permeates the law books, and thus is self-perpetuating. The average law student is indoctrinated early in his career and never thinks to question it: its characteristics, and the model of the legal system that it perpetuates, are all he knows. Legal science has been subjected to direct attack and to subversion from many sides. Its critics have tried to introduce consideration of concrete problems, to see that the existence of a subconscious and of intuition are taken into account, to bring nonlegal materials to bear on the legal consideration of social problems, and to involve legal scholars in the conscious pursuit of socioeconomic objectives. Nevertheless, the average civil lawyer still forms his own ideas of the law according to the teach-

ings of legal science. Some of the consequences of these attitudes will be described in subsequent chapters.

Although the common law world has seen occasional brief trends toward the kind of thinking that characterizes legal science, it has never really caught on here. Legal science is a creation of the professors—it smells of the lamp—and our judge-dominated law is fundamentally inhospitable to it. Common law judges are problem solvers rather than theoreticians, and the civil law emphasis on scientism, system-building, formalism, and the like gets in the way of effective problem solving. It also diminishes the role of the judge in the legal process, to the advantage of the legislator and the scholar. Both sociological jurisprudence—which is the opposite of abstraction, formalism, and purism—and legal realism—which rejects scientism and system-building—emphasize the difficulty and the importance of focusing on the judicial process. Both have flourished in the common law world, and particularly in the United States.

It is true that the famous case method of instruction, which is a creation of law professors in the United States, originated under the influence of German legal science; the idea was that decisions of courts, being sources of law, should be studied as data with the aim of deriving principles of law from them and finally arranging them into a coherent system. The end product of this line of thought in the United States was *The Restatement of the Law* (prepared mainly by professors), and its publication provided the occasion for a thorough, devastating attack by the legal realists. Since that attack, legal science has been essentially discredited in the United States, and the emphasis in legal education has subtly shifted. Cases are still studied, but they are no longer studied as the data of legal science. Instead, they are seen as convenient records of concrete social problems and as convenient examples of how the legal process operates.

The basic difference is epitomized in another quotation from the German legal scientist Rudolph Sohm: "A rule of law may be worked out either by developing the consequences that it involves, or by developing the wider principles that it presupposes.... The more important of these two methods of procedure is the second, i.e. the method by which, from given rules of law, we ascertain the major

premises they presuppose.... The law is thus enriched, and enriched by a purely scientific method." An American legal realist would resist the implication that rules of law should be the principal objects of his study or the suggestion that there are only these two ways of studying them. But if pushed to Sohm's choice, most law professors, judges, and lawyers in the United States would easily and quickly choose the first of his two methods. Most civil lawyers would still choose the second.

# XI

## THE GENERAL PART

THE ACCEPTED major classification of law within the civil law tradition is into public law and private law. Within private law there are two main fields: civil law and commercial law. Technically, the civil law (which is the modern descendant of Roman civil law) includes only the law of persons (natural and legal), the family, inheritance, property, and obligations. This is roughly the same subject matter as that covered in the *Institutes* of Justinian and the civil codes of the nineteenth century. The firm belief that these subjects, which seem quite disparate to a common lawyer, constitute a coherent body of interrelated legal principles and institutions is itself one of the distinguishing features of the civil law tradition. The principal operating legal concepts, the basic structure of the law, and the principal legal institutions are all directly drawn from or developed by analogy to the civil law. The apparatus of legal scholarship owes its origins to scholars of the civil law, and the systematic conceptual structure developed for this field has eventually been adapted to all the other fields. It is still generally believed that it is the function of the civil law scholar to develop general theories of law that are valid for the entire legal order. The growth of public law resulting from the vast increase in state activity in this century has not shaken this attitude. Civil law is still fundamental law. It is studied first, and subsequent study builds on it. It forms the matrix of thought of the lawyer in the civil law tradition.

In addition to the formal sources of the civil law, typically contained in a civil code and supplementary legislation, there is an overlay of concepts and principles derived primarily from legal scholarship. These concepts and principles and the system they form carry the great weight of scholarly authority described in Chapter IX. Although many of these concepts and principles have never existed as such in the positive civil law, they have been introduced into the legal order

by scholars, under the influence of legal science, as general legal truths derived by the scientific method from the positive law.

This superstructure of derived concepts and principles typically appears in three distinct but closely related contexts in the civil law tradition: (1) the *allgemeiner Teil*, or general part, of the German Civil Code of 1896 and other civil codes that follow the German pattern; (2) the set of basic notions on which scholars build extremely complex and sophisticated general theories of law; and (3) the content of the "introduction to law" that is taught to students at the beginning of their legal education. These three have tended to merge in those nations in which civil codes have been adopted or extensively revised under the impact of German legal science of the late nineteenth century. Even though such nations have not always copied the German civil code, there has been a strong tendency to make their own codes more "scientific." The extent to which evolution toward a "scientific" civil code has taken place thus determines the degree to which the positive law, the basic elements of accepted general theories of law, and the introductory or "general part" of courses and treatises on civil law employ the same concepts and principles. As a rule, the positive law is a good deal less "scientific," in this sense, than the law taught and written by the scholars.

The best way to capture some of the flavor of the "general part" of the civil law is to examine the "general part" of a more or less typical textbook for a civil law course. For this purpose we will sample the contents of the "preliminary notions" and "general part" of a respected elementary work (which shall remain anonymous) on private law. Although this work is not identical to similar books on French or German or Italian civil law, the pattern and the basic concepts are representative of the sort of thinking we are trying to describe.

The book begins with some "preliminary notions," the first of which is "the legal order." We are told that "no society ... is able to live in an orderly way without an aggregate of rules governing the relations among the persons who compose the group (*ubi societas ibi ius*) and individuals who are charged with enforcing their observance." Applying this observation to the state, "we ... establish the necessity both for an aggregate of norms that regulate the relations among citizens and

for ... organs and institutions that ... enforce observance of the norms established by the state." [It will be observed that this definition of the legal order, limited to rules, or norms, and institutions for their enforcement, omits processes. This is a typical traditional approach. The legal order is seen as something static. Law is viewed not as a process for the perception and resolution of problems, but as a set of established rules and institutions. Instead of studying how such institutions perceive and resolve problems, or how they make, interpret, and apply the law, the doctrine focuses on the substantive content of the existing rules as its major object of study.]

The author begins his examination of the first component of the legal order in this way: "The legal norm ... is ... a command addressed to the individual by which a determined conduct ... is imposed on him." [Actually, not all norms command; the text statement is inaccurate. There are many norms, particularly in the field of private law, that merely state the legal consequence of a state of fact: e.g. if a person dies intestate, half of his property passes to his children.] Many norms, including all those of private law, not only require or prohibit, but "correlatively attribute to another person a power." The debtor is told to pay the debt, and the creditor is given the power to obtain payment. Hence the distinction between objective law and subjective right. "Objective law is the rule to which the individual must make his conduct conform; subjective right is the power of the individual that is derived from the norm." Objective law can be distinguished into natural law and positive law. "Our study is directed exclusively toward positive law." [Here are two very significant and ideologically loaded fundamental notions. The first is that of the "subjective right." In private law, this is the foundation of a legal system in which private, individual rights, i.e., property, contract, personal, and family rights, exist. The second is the rejection of "natural law," and hence of any normative system external to the state by which the validity of the positive law can be judged.]

The legal norm is more than mere advice; to the precept is joined a threat of "an evil administered by ... the state" if it is not observed. The nature of this sanction distinguishes the legal norm from rules of custom, rules of etiquette, religious norms, and moral norms, whose

nonobservance leads to other kinds of consequences (social disapproval, pangs of conscience). The legal norm is also general; its command is not addressed to specific individuals but to a model "fact situation": the debtor who does not pay is liable for damages. If a concrete fact corresponds to this model, e.g. Smith does not pay his debt to Jones, then the effects established by the norm follow, i.e. Smith is liable to Jones for damages. [The reader will recognize that the traditional view of the judicial function described earlier is implicit in this statement. Once the facts of the case are found, the judge compares them with the model fact situations in the legal norms, selects the norm whose model corresponds to the facts of the case, and applies the consequence stated in that norm.] One difficulty with the model fact situation is that occasionally the application of the abstract norm to the concrete case "gives place to consequences that offend the sense of justice." Equity is the power to vary application of the norm; it is "the justice of the individual case." But "the legal order frequently sacrifices the justice of the individual case to the demands of certainty in the law, inasmuch as it is believed that subjecting the legal order to the subjective valuation of the judge is dangerous; it is better that individuals know in advance the precepts they must observe and the consequences of nonobservance (the principle of certainty of law)." [See Chapter VIII, above.]

These "preliminary notions" having been described, the author now moves to "the general part" of the civil law. He first distinguishes public law from private law: "The first governs the organization of the state and the other public entities ... and the relations between them and the citizen, relations in which the state and the public entities are in a position of supremacy with respect to the citizen, who is ... in a state of subjection and subordination. ... The private law regulates the relations among citizens. ... A characteristic of private law, in contrast to public law, is thus equality of position among subjects." [Compare the discussion of the public law–private law dichotomy in Chapter XIV, below.] At this point the discussion turns exclusively to private law. The author points out that private law norms are either dispositive or imperative. "The first can be modified by private arrangements or agreements; the second, insofar as they refer to the pro-

tection of fundamental social interests, are not subject to modification by individuals."

Next comes a discussion of the sources of law, i.e. of legal norms, which are said to be statutes, regulations, and custom, in that order. [See Chapter IV, above.] This is followed by a discussion of the temporal effect of legal norms: rules for determining when statutes shall take effect, methods of abrogation, the rule against retroactivity, and the effect of a change in a statute on partly completed or continuing states of fact. Then the author discusses interpretation of the legal norm, ending with a brief discussion of "the conflict of laws in space," which shows how to determine what legal norms apply when those of two or more nations are possibly applicable.

The author then turns from the legal norm to the legal relation. "Human relations can be of various kinds: they can be inspired by affection, by sentiment, by friendship, by interest, by conviviality, by cultural interests, etc. Everyone instinctively grasps the difference between those relations and that which exists between me and my debtor. This relation is regulated by the law, which attributes to me the power (subjective right) to obtain payment of the debt, and puts on my debtor the obligation to pay. Thus the legal relation is the relation between two subjects regulated by law. When one wishes to allude to the persons who have put a legal relation into effect (for example, a contract), one uses the expression parties. Opposed to the concept of parties is that of third persons. The third person is, in general, one not a party and not subject to a legal relation. It is a general rule that the legal relation does not produce effects either in favor of or against third persons (*res inter alios acta tertio neque prodest, neque nocet*)." [This rule is subject to so many exceptions that its usefulness is questionable; actually there are many situations in which the private legal relation does affect the legal interests of third persons. The tendency in the general part to overstate general propositions and to submerge exceptions is here clearly illustrated. Leaving aside the inaccuracy of the generalization, note that there is no reference to the very interesting question of whether, and if so under what circumstances, third persons *should* be affected by private legal relations. The tenets of traditional scholarship—particularly the belief that only legal

considerations, narrowly defined, are of interest to the legal scholar—
exclude these matters from discussion. The rule is stated as the product
of scientific investigation. No normative judgment on it is expressly
made, but the methods and objectives of legal science and the authority
of the doctrine give it a normative impact. In terms of the "is" and the
"ought," the statement in question misstates the "is," avoids discussing
the "ought," and implies a normative judgment that the misstated "is"
is the desirable rule.]

In general, the term "subjective right" is used to indicate the legal
interest of the person who has the benefit of a legal relation in private
law. "The ultimate end that the norm seeks is always the protection
of general interests. In many cases, however (and it is the rule in
private law), it is the view that the best way to pursue this end consists in promoting individual interests, in stimulating individual initiative. The legal order recognizes the interests of the individual and
seeks to effect the realization of his intention. Therefore the subjective
right is defined as the primacy of intention, as the power to act for
the satisfaction of one's own interests, protected by the legal order."
[Here again we encounter the fundamental importance of the subjective right in private law. In addition, the reference to "the primacy
of intention" conceals a long, voluminous scholarly debate. Some
argued that private rights could be created, and private obligations
imposed, only with the conscious assent of the individuals concerned.
They were seeking the ultimate source of private legal relations, and
they found it in the individual intention, or will. The *Willenstheorie*
and the rule, criticized above, concerning the effects of legal relations
on third persons, are logically related to each other. If the will or
volition of the individual is taken as the true source of the legal obligation, then it seems right to conclude that one who has not expressed
the will or volition to enter into the relation—i.e. one who is not a
party to it—cannot be subjected to the obligations and cannot claim
the benefits of it. (The parties to the contract are bound by it only because they voluntarily entered into the contract.) But if the *Willenstheorie* is abandoned, and if the view is generally taken that the true
source of the rights and obligations arising out of the legal relation
is the positive legal order itself, then the third persons rule does not

necessarily, or even logically, follow. Instead, one is freer to adopt a more eclectic approach to the problem of whether and under what circumstances third persons should be legally affected by the agreement of the parties to the legal relation. The author does not discuss the point.]

The holder of a subjective right is not required to compensate others for any prejudice that the exercise of the right may cause to them, except where he abuses the right. [The criticisms made above of the rule that third persons are unaffected by a private legal relation apply to one interpretation of this statement. If it means anything, it is far from accurate, and it embodies a set of value judgments that the author never discusses. Is it true that the holder of the right is free to exercise it to the injury of others, so long as he does not "abuse" the privilege? Why? We could argue that the statement is nothing more than a tautology. If we say that the holder of a subjective right is liable to others for the exercise of that right only if he abuses it, then we have said that he is not liable for exercise of the right except when he is liable for the exercise of the right.] In some jurisdictions, such as France, courts use a general doctrine of scholarly origin to define "abuse of right." In others it is thought dangerous "to entrust the determination of the limits of the subjective right to the discretionary and variable criteria employed by judges." In the interest of certainty, then, the judge has this power only in selected, legislatively defined cases.

"The first and fundamental division of subjective rights" is into "*absolute rights*, which guarantee to the owner a power that he can exercise against all others (*erga omnes*), and *relative rights*, which give him a power that he can exercise only against one or more determined persons. Typical absolute rights are the *real rights*, that is to say, rights in a thing. These attribute sovereignty, either full (ownership) or limited (real right in another's thing), over a thing to the owner. The immediate relation between the man and the thing stands out clearly, and is effective without need for the cooperation of others. Other subjects must merely abstain from interfering in the peaceful exercise of this sovereignty. In an obligatory relation, however [where only relative rights are involved], the conduct of another subject who

is held to a determined conduct is of primary importance. The category of relative rights coincides with that of *rights of credit* (which are also called *personal rights* in contrast to real rights); that of the absolute rights includes not only the real rights but also the so-called *rights of personality* (right to a name, to one's image, and so on). The reverse, whether of the right of credit or of the real right, is the *duty*: negative duty of abstention in the real right, and duty (more precisely, *obligation*) of one or more determined persons in the right of credit.

"The legal relation is constituted when the subject acquires the subjective right. Acquisition indicates the association of a right with a person, who then becomes its owner: in substance, a subjective right becomes a part of the person's patrimony. The acquisition can be of two kinds: by *original title*, when the subjective right arises in favor of a person without being transmitted from another; and by *derivative title*, when the right is transmitted from one person to another. In acquisition by derivative title, one observes this phenomenon: the right that appertains to one person passes to another. This phenomenon is called *succession*. It indicates a change in the subject of a legal relation. In acquisition by derivative title, the new subject has the same right that the preceding titleholder had, or a right derived from it. This justifies the following rules: (1) The new titleholder cannot exercise a right greater than the one the preceding titleholder had (*nemo plus iuris quan ipse habet transferre potest*); (2) The validity and efficacy of the new title depend as a rule on the validity and efficacy of the preceding title." [Here again, these "rules" are subject to so many qualifications and exceptions that their usefulness as rules is dubious. The transferee of a right may get more or less than the transferor had, and the validity and efficacy of the new title can depend on factors other than the validity and efficacy of the preceding title. And as is often the case, these "rules" embody normative judgments about a variety of undisclosed issues.]

The author next turns to "the subject of the legal relation," discussing the legal characteristics of physical persons and legal persons (e.g. companies, foundations). Then, under the heading "the object of the legal relation," he discusses the legal concept of a thing (corporeal and incorporeal, movable and immovable, fungible and non-

fungible, divisible and indivisible, consumable and nonconsumable, and so on).

Having discussed the basic characteristics of the legal relation in private law, typified by the subjective right and the subjective duty, the author turns to the proudest achievement of the civil law doctrine: the "juridical act." [This is the archetypal product of the methods and objectives of legal science discussed in Chapter X. Whole libraries of books and articles have been written on it. In some nations the notion has been employed in legislation (for example, in the German civil code). In others it is found only in the doctrine. But in any civil law nation it functions in two major ways: as a central concept in the systematic reconstruction of the legal order produced and perpetuated by scholars; and, together with the concept of the subjective right, as the vehicle for assertion and perpetuation of the role of individual autonomy in the law.]

The concept of the juridical act is based on another concept, the "legal fact." It will be recalled that the legal norm contains a statement of a model fact situation and a legal result. If the concrete facts that fit the model fact situation occur, then the legal result becomes operative. A legal fact is an event (e.g. birth or death of a person, a contract) that fits a model fact situation and that therefore has certain legal consequences. It is a legally relevant fact, as distinguished from those that have no legal relevance. Legal facts include "natural facts that come into being without the participation of our intention (the death of a person from sickness, an earthquake), as well as acts deliberately and voluntarily performed by men." Thus the distinction of legal facts into two categories: legal fact in the strict sense (i.e. mere legal fact) and deliberate, voluntary legal acts.

"Legal acts are distinguished into two large categories: acts that conform to the requirements of the legal order (*licit acts*) and acts that are performed in violation of legal duties and that produce injury to the subjective right of others (*illicit acts*). The licit acts are subdivided into *operations*, which consist of modifications of the external world (for example, the taking of possession, the construction of a ship), and *declarations*, which are acts directed toward communicating one's thought, one's state of mind, or one's intention to others.

The acts intended to communicate one's thought or one's state of mind are called *declarations of knowledge* (for example, notification); the acts intended to communicate one's intention constitute *juridical acts.* These last have been the object of significant doctrinal elaboration; as to the others, which are also called *legal acts in the strict sense,* the single point of certainty seems to be the nonapplicability of principles relative to the juridical act. In general, one can say that legal acts in the strict sense are acts that presuppose intention and deliberation in the actor, but not the intention to produce a legal effect: this is attached automatically by the legal order to the performance of the act. For example, if a person declares in writing in an unequivocal manner that he is the father of a child conceived out of wedlock, the child has a right to support according to the civil code, even if the declarer did not have any intention to attribute such a right to him by the act of declaration.

"Among legal acts, the juridical act is of fundamental importance. In fact, it constitutes the most complete and interesting expression of legal activity. To understand the notion of the juridical act well, it is desirable to move to an empirical demonstration. He who executes a will or the parties who enter into a contract intend to produce legal effects: to distribute one's goods among the persons that the testator will leave at the moment of his death or to transfer by sale the ownership of a thing in exchange for the price, and so forth. It is easy, therefore, to understand the definition given by the prevailing doctrine: the juridical act is a declaration of intention directed toward legal effects that the legal order recognizes and guarantees. And it is this direction of the intention toward legal effects that constitutes the characteristic element of the concept of the juridical act, and distinguishes it from legal acts in the strict sense, which—as we have seen—are also voluntary and deliberate acts, but produce their effects without requiring that the intention of the person who performs them be directed toward the production of these specified effects. These legal effects at which the parties aim are recognized and guaranteed by the legal order: this distinguishes the juridical act from illicit acts which—as we have seen—violate duties established by the legal order. The juridical act is a general figure elaborated by the writers drawing

upon the study of particular legal figures (contracts, will, and so on). These figures present common characteristics. The fundamental characteristic consists in the fact that these are expressions of private autonomy, of the power that the legal order recognizes in individuals to regulate their own interests. This power is not, however, unlimited: the liberty of the subject to put transactions into being is subordinated to observance of rules dictated by the order, which establishes a series of burdens and limits. (For example, if one wishes to transfer real property, it is necessary to use the written form.) Above all, it is required that the purpose to which the act is directed be recognized as worthy of protection by the legal order. The study of the general theory of the juridical act is very important. Since the legal order recognizes the power of the will of individuals in regulating their own interests in the field of private law, the greater part of legal activity consists of juridical acts."

[The preceding paragraph illustrates several characteristics of legal science: the emphasis placed in the traditional doctrine on "private" juridical acts and the "private" legal relations arising out of them; the highly systematic methods of legal science ("the juridical act is a general figure elaborated by the writers drawing upon the study of particular legal figures"); and the remoteness of the doctrine from concrete problems. How, for example, does one go about determining whether a specific act is or should be considered "worthy of protection by the legal order"? Who decides, and by what criteria? How does the legal process place this kind of limit on private autonomy?]

Next follows a description of the various types of juridical acts (unilateral or multilateral, *inter vivos* or at death, gratuitous or onerous, and so on). Then the author begins an extensive discussion of the elements of the juridical act. "The elements of the juridical act are divided into *essential elements*, without which the act is void, and *accidental elements*, which the parties are free to include or not. The essential elements are called *general* if they apply to every type of act (such as intention, cause); *particular* if they refer to the particular type being considered. Thus in a sale, besides intention and cause, the thing and the price are essential." Then follow discussions of the general essential elements (intention and cause) and of the general accidental

elements (condition, time limit, mode). And finally come discussions of interpretation and effects, and of the consequences of voidness and voidability of the juridical act.

The general part of this manual then closes with brief general discussions of the judicial protection of subjective rights and the proof of legal facts in civil actions. The general part is contained in 236 pages —more than a fourth of the entire volume. More than a hundred of those pages deal with the juridical act. Nowhere in the general part is there a discussion of specific subjective rights or specific legal institutions. The progress is from the more general and abstract to the less general but still abstract. The discussion of specific subjective rights and specific legal institutions later in the volume goes on within the conceptual structure established in the general part. More important, the later discussion has the same tone and style; the emphasis is on inclusive definitions, clean conceptual distinctions, and broad general rules. There is no testing of definitions, distinctions, and rules against reality. Indeed, the tone set trains the lawyer to make the concrete facts fit into the conceptual structure. The tendency is to preserve the rule from the exception, to smooth out the rough spots.

The law of the general part is thus doctrinal law; it is a law purely of the scholars, and if we encounter it in the enacted, living law of a civil law nation, as in Germany, it is because the lawmaker has chosen to put the doctrine into statutory form. The civil codes that preceded the German BGB naturally contain no similar general part, but even those that followed it have, on the whole, preferred to maintain a formal separation between the scientific work of the scholar and the lawmaking work of the legislator. The result, in most modern civil codes, is that the legislation reflects but does not expressly embody the general doctrinal scheme here described. However, it is enacted, interpreted, and applied by men whose minds have been trained in the doctrinal pattern and to whom the scheme here described seems basic, obvious, and true. The conceptual structure and its inherent, unstated assumptions about law and the legal process constitute a kind of classroom law that hovers over the legal order, deeply affecting the way lawyers, legislators, administrators, and judges think and work.

Attempts to introduce a similar systematic reconstruction of the

basic elements of positive law in the common law world have, on the whole, been failures. There was a time, toward the end of the nineteenth century, when legal scholars in England and the United States sought to emulate German legal science. The introduction of the case method of instruction in the Harvard Law School during the 1870's was based partly on the assumptions of legal science. Early in this century English and American analytical jurists produced a good deal of scholarship that resembles the work of legal science in a number of ways, and a revival of analytical jurisprudence is now going on in the common law world. The ambitious undertaking called *The Restatement of the Law*, begun in the 1920's and carried on by a group of outstanding professors at major American law schools, has had much in common with the civil law doctrine typified by the discussion of the general part described in this chapter. But there have also been a number of counter-influences: the impact of sociological jurisprudence and of legal realism, the lesser role of legal scholars and their work, the dominance of the problem-solving judge, and the different style and objectives of American legal education are among them. Most thoughtful legal scholars in the United States and England recognize the value of order and system, and they long, at least occasionally, for the introduction of a similar degree of order into our law. At the same time, most of them believe that the price is likely to be too high. They fear that this kind of order costs more in terms of sensitivity to the needs of a highly complex, constantly changing society than people should be willing to pay. Even those who are willing to pay that price lack the power within the legal process that is needed to establish a doctrinal system. They are teacher-scholars, and the protagonist of our legal process is still the judge.

# XII

# THE LEGAL PROCESS

I N THIS chapter we will be concerned with who does what in the legal system and why; we want to try to understand the basic division of labor in the legal process. Our task is considerably complicated by the fact that there is a substantial disparity between generally accepted and frequently repeated ideas about the legal process on the one hand, and how the process actually works on the other. The generally accepted folklore, derived from revolutionary ideology and the dogmas of legal science, has an important effect on the way people act, but does not accurately represent their actions.

According to the folklore, the legal scholar does the basic thinking for the legal system. He is constantly improving the state of legal science by discovering and organizing fundamental, objective legal truth on which other elements of the legal process can then build. He publishes the results of his work in books and articles called "the doctrine," and teaches the basic principles of the doctrine to students in the universities. The doctrine is the basis of the legal system, and is thought to represent objectively stated scientific truth. The doctrine is not law in action, and indeed the scholar would regard such matters as diversionary. He does not consider it his function to enact statutes (as distinguished from drafting codes or other systematic legislation) or to decide cases. He fears that if he became involved in these activities, he might lose his objectivity and perspective, and in any event would be misusing his time, which should be spent on more fundamental, and hence more valuable work. For a slightly different set of reasons, he believes it important to avoid focusing on social, economic, political, or other nonlegal matters, or committing himself to a particular theory of justice. He believes that he should be uncommitted to any ideology or any objective other than truth—a pure scientist, distinct from the legislators and judges, whom he sees as, at most, engineers.

The legislator, representing the people and operating in the area of practical politics, has quite different obligations. It is he who must relate economic and social demands to the legislative process, producing laws that respond to people's needs and desires. In enacting such legislation, however, the legislator must never lose sight of the basic truth of the sort provided for him by the legal scientist. He will find this truth not only in the doctrine, but also in systematic legislation enacted by earlier legislators with the assistance of scholars, particularly in the basic codes of the jurisdiction. Thus new legislation will employ the concepts and institutions and follow the organization established by the scholars and embodied in earlier systematic legislation. The primary function of legislation is to supplement the codes where necessary and to perfect prior legislation, including that of the codes, where it is shown by the continuing investigations of legal scientists to be defective. If the legislature follows the instructions of scholars it will tend to avoid the danger of incompleteness or lack of clarity and to produce legislation that is systematic and, according to the criteria of legal science, valid. Legal scientists will criticize legislation, but not on the basis of its probable social or economic effects. They will discuss its consistency with the tenets of legal science, the quality of its draftsmanship, and its compatibility with the established conceptual system.

Judges, according to the folklore, are merely the operators of a machine designed by scientists and built by legislators, and indeed, one commonly finds judges referred to in the literature of the civil law world as "operators of the law." When a case comes before a judge for decision, he extracts the relevant facts from the raw problem, characterizes the legal question that these facts present, finds the appropriate legislative provision, and applies it to the problem. Unless the legal scientist and the legislator have failed in their functions, the task of the judge is a simple one; there is only one correct solution, and there is no room for the exercise of judicial discretion. If the judge has difficulty finding the applicable provision or interpreting and applying that provision to the fact situation, then one of the following men must be at fault: the judge, because he does not know how to follow clear instructions; the legislator, because he failed to draft

clearly stated and clearly applicable legislation; or the legal scholar, either because he has failed to perceive certain defects in the legal science he teaches or because he has failed properly to instruct the judge on how to apply the statutes. No other explanation is permissible. If everyone did his job right, the judge would have no difficulty in finding, interpreting, and applying the applicable law. Such difficult cases are, therefore, thought to be rare pathological examples. They are not seen to impair the general validity of the working model of the legal process. In the pathological case, it is desirable that the legal scientist immediately examine and propose a remedy for consideration by the legislator. There is consequently bound to be a certain amount of doctrinal discussion of problems of interpretation and application of the law so long as the legal order remains imperfect. Pending action by the legislator, of course, judges should be, and actually are, influenced by doctrinal interpretation.

Hovering over the entire legal process is a brooding anxiety about certainty. The legal scholar seeks to make the law more certain by making it systematic. Certainty requires that the law be completely, coherently, and clearly stated by the legislature, and only by the legislature. Judges are restricted to interpretation and application of "the law" in the interest of certainty, and prior judicial decisions are not "law." Judges are also denied the power to temper the rigor of a rule in a hard case. All nonlegal considerations must be excluded from the law in the interest of certainty. Considerations of justice or other ends of the law must be excluded for the same reason. Hard cases, unjust decisions, unrealistic decisions, are regrettable, but they are the price one has to pay for certainty.

This is the folklore of the working legal process in the civil law tradition. Although many participants in such a legal process believe in and strive to act according to this model, there are a number of ways in which practice differs from theory. First, legal science does not speak with one voice. It is common for different schools of thought to be at war with each other over matters that are fundamental to the legal structure, as well as over the merits and defects of specific pieces of legislation or specific judicial decisions. In fact, at any given moment one can find within the scholarly community of the civil law

world many different points of view about most legal problems. Even within the relatively monolithic tradition of pure legal science, a little investigation reveals that basic propositions supposed to be objective actually conceal fairly important value judgments. Jurists of the left have tirelessly and shrilly complained of the ideological bias of European legal science for over a century. Much of the supposedly disinterested legal scholarship that has emerged in the civil law world in the nineteenth and twentieth centuries is seen by them to be a kind of apologia for the institutions and values of nineteenth-century bourgeois liberalism.

Although the legislature tries to provide a clear, systematic legislative response for every problem that may arise, legislative practice falls far short of this objective. As a result, judges have a lot of interpreting to do. They frequently find themselves confronted by problems in which the only applicable legislation is so general as to be useless, is unclear or contradictory in application, or is obviously the product of a legislature that did not foresee the problem now facing the judge. Since in all jurisdictions the judge is required to decide the case before him and cannot give up on the ground that the law is unclear, judges continually make law in civil law jurisdictions. Given inadequate legislative direction on the one hand, and the command to decide the case, in any event, on the other, they improvise. The judge may try to show how his decision proceeds logically from the rule stated by the legislature. Even when a judge believes this to be the case, however, he is still making law. In nations with old codes, the cumulative effect of this kind of judicial lawmaking is particularly obvious. In France, for example, where the Code Napoléon is still in force, the law of torts is almost entirely the product of judicial decisions based on a few very general provisions of the code.

The effect of this kind of lawmaking is compounded by the fact that decisions of the high courts, and some decisions of lower courts, are regularly published (although often in truncated form, frequently lacking the full statement of the facts we are used to in our own judicial opinions), and are cited before courts in subsequent cases. The way of a lawyer with a difficult legal problem is made much easier if he can find a reported judicial decision interpreting the statute

in question. The same, of course, is true for a judge. It is true that he is, at least in theory, free to ignore the prior decision if he thinks it wrong. But in fact, if the prior decision is by a court above his in the judicial hierarchy, he will probably follow it even if he doubts its correctness, because he does not wish his ruling to be reversed. Where the prior decision is one pronounced by the Supreme Court of Cassation or its equivalent, one of whose historical functions has been to provide a final authoritative interpretation of the statutes, the lower judge will probably follow it. The fiction is that he cites and follows the prior decision because it agrees with his own thinking about how the law should be interpreted and applied. The fact is that he follows it for reasons that are inconsistent with the prevailing model of the legal process.

The gap between the model of the legal process that has grown out of the civil law tradition on the one hand, and what people and institutions actually do on the other, is widely appreciated within the civil law world. Although a great deal of scholarly energy and ingenuity is devoted to proving that the gap is not really there, a growing number of scholars, legislators, and judges have reacted against the traditional model. There has been no revolution in legal thought as drastic as that produced by the legal realism movement in the United States (and, it should be noted, in Scandinavia), but there is a growing tendency to blame the traditional model for failures of justice, popular dissatisfaction with the legal system, and the dragging pace of social and economic development. There is a growing tendency to question the relevance of the traditional, doctrinally oriented system of legal education, and of the products of that system, to the process of decision-making in the public and private sectors of national life. The ability of scholars working in the tradition of pure legal science to design a satisfactory law machine is in doubt. The dogma of legislative infallibility has been fundamentally shaken. The image of the judicial function steadily expands. Lawyers in other parts of the world are asking themselves whether ideas about the legal process that emerged from the peculiar conditions of revolutionary France and nineteenth-century Germany are necessarily valid for other nations in other times. The folklore is clearly losing its power, but until some

new, acceptable, coherent view of the legal process appears to replace it, it will continue to occupy the field. It is still the residual model of the legal process, and even scholars who recognize that this model is not working spend more effort trying to perfect its basic design than in trying to design a better model.

One reason why a new model has not appeared may be the implied threat it poses to continued domination of the legal process by scholars. Although it would be grotesque to suggest the existence of some sort of collusion among scholars, the fact is that the model of the legal process we have been discussing in this chapter was created, and has been happily perpetuated by scholars. Attempts in the civil law world to introduce sociological jurisprudence, the jurisprudence of interests, and legal realism—to mention only three different coherent attacks on the traditional model—have not gone very far. These schools of thought have not been refuted, or even ignored; they simply have not penetrated deeply into the legal consciousness. Each of these three would redefine the judicial function to emphasize the great power and responsibility exercised by judges. Each would, in a sense, aggrandize the role of the judge, and at least indirectly diminish that of the scholar. All have failed to dislodge the traditional model, which glorifies the scholar, flatters the legislator, and demeans the judge.

# XIII

## THE DIVISION OF JURISDICTION

THE TYPICAL common law country has a unified court system that might be represented as a pyramid with a single supreme court at the apex. Regardless of the number of different kinds of courts and of the way jurisdiction is divided among them in lower parts of the pyramid, every case is at least potentially subject to final scrutiny by a supreme court. The decision in a criminal action, in a private action between parties to an automobile accident or contract, on a complaint by a citizen concerning the legality of administrative action, on an argument about constitutional rights, and on appeal from an award of compensation by an administrative tribunal—all may be reviewed by the same high court. It seems entirely natural to us that the ultimate power to review the legality of administrative action and the constitutionality of legislative action, as well as to hear and decide the great range of civil and criminal disputes, should be lodged in a supreme court.

Matters are typically quite different in the civil law world. There it is usual to find two or more separate sets of courts, each with its own jurisdiction, its own hierarchy of tribunals, its own judiciary, and its own procedure, all existing within the same nation. A case falling within one jurisdiction will be immune from consideration, whether at the trial or at the appellate level, in the others. If the typical common law judicial system can be represented as a pyramid, the typical civil law judicial system must be visualized as a set of two or more distinct structures.

The most important of these jurisdictions, the one that impinges most obviously and frequently on the life of the ordinary citizen, is the system of so-called "ordinary" courts. Such courts, manned by "ordinary" judges, hear and decide the great range of civil and criminal litigation. They are the modern descendants of the various civil courts that existed in Europe during the period of the jus commune

and that were an object of revolutionary reform. When one speaks of civil law judges, one usually means the ordinary judiciary. The theory of the separation of powers, insofar as it concerns "the judiciary," applies to the ordinary judiciary. It is the ordinary judges whose primary concern is the interpretation and application of the basic codes. When, with the rise of the modern nation-state, the administration of justice was taken out of ecclesiastical, local, and private hands and was nationalized, the ordinary courts became the principal instrument of the state's monopoly on the administration of justice. The legislation was given a monopoly on the nationalized process of lawmaking. The ordinary judiciary was given a monopoly on the nationalized process of adjudication.

The ordinary jurisdiction, as it exists today in France, for example, is really a composite of a number of jurisdictions having separate historical origins. At the core is the sort of adjudication performed during the period of the jus commune by local courts in the common run of secular civil and criminal disputes. Later, as the civil jurisdiction of the ecclesiastical tribunals gradually diminished and finally disappeared, the power formerly exercised by them was absorbed by the civil courts. The commercial courts, originally established by merchants to adjudicate their disputes, eventually were nationalized and incorporated into the judicial system. In France and a few other nations, commercial courts still maintain a separate identity at the trial level, but they are subject to the same appellate jurisdiction as ordinary trial courts. In others, such as Italy, the evolution has gone a step further; commercial jurisdiction has become part of the ordinary jurisdiction at every level, and separate commercial courts no longer exist.

At the apex of the system of ordinary courts in France, and in many nations have followed the French model, is the Supreme Court of Cassation, a body that, as we have seen, originated as a nonjudicial tribunal, created to provide authoritative answers to questions of interpretation of statutes referred to it by the ordinary judges. Even though this nonjudicial tribunal has become the highest court in the ordinary judiciary, its actual jurisdiction still shows the signs of its origins. In Italy, for example, the Supreme Court of Cassation hears

only questions of "interpretation and application of the law." Hence, a party to an action can have a hearing before the Court of Cassation only if he can phrase his objection so as to call into question the way the lower court interpreted or applied a statute, a regulation, or custom. An argument that the lower court misconstrued or misapplied a contract, a will, or a corporate charter is not a question of interpretation of "the law" (although often it can easily be converted into one), and hence cannot be made before the Court of Cassation. Arguments about the facts of the case are also excluded; the only permissible questions are questions of law.

Further, the Court of Cassation decides only the question of law that has been referred to it; it does not decide the case. If it finds that the lower court's interpretation was correct, it says so. If it finds that the lower court made an error in interpretation, it explains what the correct interpretation is, quashes the decision, and orders the lower court (or another court at the same level) to reconsider the case according to the Court of Cassation's authoritative interpretation.

The ordinary jurisdiction in a typical civil law nation thus combines elements of jurisdiction formerly distributed among the civil courts of the period of the jus commune, the ecclesiastical courts, the commercial courts, and the special tribunal created after the French Revolution to deal with problems of interpretation of statutes. In civil (i.e. noncriminal) matters the ordinary courts apply the law found in the civil and commercial codes and in the legislation that supplements them. Their procedure in such cases is governed by the code of civil procedure. In criminal cases the courts apply the law found in the penal code and legislation supplementary to it; their procedure in such cases is governed by the code of criminal procedure. The ordinary courts also regularly apply a great deal of law that is not contained in these five basic codes and their supplementary legislation, but it is still the tendency to regard the ordinary jurisdiction and the basic codes as functionally equivalent to each other.

A typical civil law nation will also have a set of administrative courts, entirely separate and exercising an independent jurisdiction. The basic reason is, again, the revolutionary doctrine of separation of powers. One of the complaints against the judiciary (i.e. the ordinary

judiciary) in prerevolutionary France was that the judges wrongly interfered with the administrative work of the government in a variety of ways. One of the objectives of the revolutionary reforms was to deprive ordinary judges of any power to determine the legality of administrative action or to control the conduct of government officials. Just as the separation of the legislative and judicial powers denied judges any opportunity to interfere in the legislative process, so the separation of the administrative and judicial powers denied them that opportunity in the administrative process.

The notion that the legislature was to be the sole source of law meant that there could be no inherent administrative power. The administration was to function only to the extent and within the limits of the authority granted it by the lawmaker. Accordingly, every administrative act was potentially subject to the test of legality, and some body other than the judiciary—which was excluded by the doctrine of separation of powers—was needed to rule on the legality of administrative action. In France this need was met by the Council of State, which began as a body of advisers to the King and gradually became the central organ of governmental administration. To its administrative functions was added that of hearing and deciding complaints concerning the legality of administrative action, and the section of the Council of State that regularly exercised this power soon developed judicial characteristics. It has its own procedure and its own catalogue of remedies, and it has produced an immense amount of case law, which is regularly published and is regularly used by lawyers. The landmark decisions (*les grands arrêts*) of the Council of State are a principal source of French administrative law. A number of other nations, including Belgium and Italy, have followed the French model and allocated similar administrative jurisdiction to their own councils of state. In other nations, like Germany and Austria, administrative courts, as such, have been created.

The theory is that the ordinary and administrative jurisdictions are separate and exclusive, so that a case falls into one or the other, but never both. Occasionally, however, a doubtful case arises; if such a case is brought before the administrative court, for example, the defendant argues that it properly belongs in the ordinary jurisdiction. De-

spite the best efforts of scholars and legislators, no simple, infallible test has yet been devised, and accordingly the matter is settled by litigation. Three examples of the procedure for deciding this question in Europe are instructive. In Italy, the Supreme Court of Cassation is the ultimate authority on conflicts of jurisdiction between the ordinary and the administrative courts. In France the question is finally settled by a special court, called the Conflicts Tribunal. In Germany the court in which the action is brought decides whether or not it has jurisdiction. Its decision can be appealed within its jurisdiction, but it is not subject to further review.

When, after World War II, it was decided to establish rigid constitutions in Germany and Italy, some method of reviewing legislative action for constitutionality had to be found. It was clear that this power could not be exercised by the judiciary (i.e. the ordinary judiciary) without violating the doctrine of separation of powers and limiting the supremacy of the legislature. The kind of thinking that had led to the creation of a separate jurisdiction to review the legality of administrative action led the Germans and Italians to establish separate constitutional courts for this purpose. Although civil law fundamentalists have occasionally argued that these tribunals cannot really be courts or the officials who man them judges (since courts and judges, properly speaking, merely interpret and apply the law made by the legislature), this view has yielded to the kind of relaxation of principle that led people to regard the Council of State as a court and the officials who man it as judges. The principle of separation of powers and the traditional civil law image of the judicial function continue to apply to the work of the ordinary judiciary. Separate administrative and constitutional courts are not thought to violate that principle.

Consequently it is common throughout the civil law world to find separate sets of courts performing the functions that fall within unified systems in the United States and other common law nations. In some nations in Latin America, however, where the influence of the American Revolution and the public law of the United States was particularly strong at the time of independence, unified judicial systems were established. The pattern varies from one nation to another.

Where a unified judicial system exists, it reflects a more general phenomenon: the substantial influence of the North American model on Latin American public law, as compared with the minimal North American influence on Latin American private law. For reasons that will be explained in a later chapter, however, the supreme courts in such unified jurisdictions have never attained the prestige or exercised the power of the North American model.

## LEGAL CATEGORIES

IT IS OBVIOUS enough that the law can be divided in various ways to serve a variety of functions. It is equally obvious, although more difficult to demonstrate, that any division of the law is bound to shape the legal system. The conventional way of dividing the law becomes a part of the law itself, affecting the way that law is formulated and applied. Thus the manner in which the law is divided and classified will affect such activities as characterization (how shall a problem be characterized for legal treatment), teaching (what courses will make up the law school curriculum), scholarship (what are the typical fields of specialization among legal scholars), organization of law libraries (how shall books be classified), codification (what constitutes an appropriate area of the law for codification), legal writing and publishing (what will be the area of concern of a book or a legal periodical), and ordinary communication among lawyers. The generally accepted way of dividing and classifying the law in the civil law world is quite different from that to which the common lawyer has been accustomed.

One of the most characteristic aspects of the traditional civil law way of dividing law is the measurably greater degree of emphasis on, and confidence in, the validity and utility of formal definitions and distinctions. While common lawyers tend to think of the division of the law as conventional, i.e. as the product of some mixture of history, convenience, and habit, the influence of scholars, and particularly of legal science, has led civil lawyers to treat the matter of division of the law in more normative terms. As we have seen in Chapter X, definitions and categories are thought to be scientifically derivable from some kind of inherent legal reality. Once scientifically found and refined, they are incorporated into the systematic reconstruction of the law that is the subject matter of legal science. Thus the descriptive merges into the normative. The emphasis of legal scholars on system,

abstraction, formalism, and purity further amplifies the apparently authoritative impact of the distinctions and definitions of legal science. The definitions and categories become part of the systematic legal structure that is employed by legal scholars, is taught to law students, and is thereby built into the law. Their methodological utility is considered incidental to their essential validity.

The main division of law in the civil law tradition is into public law and private law. This distinction seems to most civil lawyers to be fundamental, necessary and, on the whole, evident. Treatises, monographs, and student manuals all contain discussions of the dichotomy, often in confidently dogmatic terms that put to rest incipient doubts. The European or Latin American law student, who encounters this sweeping division at the outset of his career, tends uncritically to absorb it. It quickly becomes basic to his legal outlook. Some legal scholars attack the dichotomy (which the English jurist T. E. Holland termed "the mighty cleavage") as being neither fundamental nor necessary, and certainly not clear; but such doubts seldom occur to the average civil lawyer. He knows that public law and private law are essentially different. Where classification as one or the other seems difficult, he is encouraged to blame the positive legal order for not yet adequately comprehending and articulating the true nature of the underlying reality. Fortunately, legal scholars continue to work on such problems, and eventually, he believes, legal science will make it all clear. Meanwhile statutes, decisions, and doctrine that either assume or attempt to clarify the dichotomy continue to appear, embedding it ever deeper in the law. Examining the origins and the current "crisis" of the distinction is an interesting way to learn more about the civil law tradition.

The distinction between public law and private law has a long history in the civil law tradition. There is some uncertainty about whether it first appeared in classical Roman law or only later, in the *Corpus Juris Civilis* of Justinian, but there is no doubt that the Glossators and the Commentators made the distinction in their writing and teaching. It became a part of the common store of assumptions of the jus commune, and was actively employed during the process of codification and reform in the nineteenth century. When, later in the same century,

the law was subjected to the scrutiny of legal scientists, the division between public and private law became basic to their systematic reconstruction of the legal order. The continuous history of the cleavage gave it authority and built it into the culture. Concepts that had been used by legal scholars for many centuries seemed fundamental, necessary, and evident.

Much of the force behind the public law–private law cleavage in modern European legal thought is ideological, the expression of those currents of economic, social, and political thought dominant in the seventeenth and eighteenth centuries that found expression in the civil codes of France, Austria, Italy, and Germany in the nineteenth century. This codified civil law was the heart of private law, and the dominant concepts of the codes were individual private property and individual freedom of contract. This individualistic emphasis was an expression in forensic terms of the rationalism and secular natural law of the age. The emphasis on rights of property and contract in the codes guaranteed individual rights against intrusion by the state. The civil codes were thought of as serving something like a constitutional function. Private law was that area of the law in which the sole function of government was the recognition and enforcement of private rights.

Accompanying this basic attitude were various corollary assumptions Among these were a rather primitive view of the economy, in which the principal actors were private individuals, and an extremely limited view of the appropriate sphere of government activity. Neither associations of individuals engaged in concerted activity, such as corporations and labor unions, nor broad participation by government in the economic and social life of the nation—both familiar to us in the twentieth century—was contemplated. The only actors in the legal universe were the private individual and the state, and each had its domain: private law for one and public law for the other.

In the legal scholarship of the nineteenth century this ideology was accepted, at times perhaps without question. Indeed, much of the effort of legal science went into the construction of theories that embodied, but did not directly express, the essentials of what is commonly called nineteenth-century liberalism. One of the major achievements

of the German Pandectists was to raise this ideology to a highly systematic and abstract level in the name of legal science; they did it so well that these essentially nineteenth-century attitudes have been preserved in much of the European legal scholarship of the twentieth century. The fundamental concepts of the German doctrine are juridical formulations of the role of individual autonomy in the law, and they operate in an area coterminous with that of private law.

It was a kind of negative implication of this private law ideology that an entirely different attitude was appropriate in public law matters. There the role of government was not limited to the protection of private rights; on the contrary, the driving consideration was the effectuation of the public interest by state action. Public law had, from this point of view, two major components: constitutional law in the classic sense—the law by which the governmental structure is constituted—and administrative law—the law governing the public administration and its relations with private individuals. In private legal relations the parties were equals and the state the referee. In public legal relations the state was a party, and as representative of the public interest (and successor to the prince), it was a party superior to the private individual. The development of these two quite different ideologies of private law and public law further embedded the distinction in the legal order.

It has been shown in Chapter XIII that the separation of powers doctrine necessitated the existence of two sets of courts—the administrative courts and the ordinary courts. There has been a good deal of discussion, legislation, and litigation in civil law countries about the division of jurisdiction between the two. In no country is the distinction between public law and private law entirely congruent with that between administrative and ordinary jurisdiction. (For one thing, criminal law, invariably classified as public law by Europeans, is uniformly kept in the ordinary jurisdiction.) There remains, however, a rough correspondence between private law and ordinary jurisdiction, since in Europe the ordinary courts have traditionally been the ones in which controversies about private rights have been decided. This does not mean that all public law questions (other than criminal matters) are exclusively in the administrative jurisdiction and that all private law

questions (in addition to criminal matters) are in the ordinary juris-diction. The matter is much more complicated than that, but the pub-lic law–private law distinction is closely related to the phenomenon of the separate system of administrative courts on the Continent and elsewhere in the civil law world.

Thus a variety of influences combine to give the distinction a special importance in the civil law tradition: (1) scholars, particularly legal scientists, with their emphasis on systematic conceptual structures and their ability to convert the descriptive to the normative; (2) tradition, since the distinction figures importantly for at least fourteen centuries; (3) ideology, deeply embedded in the ostensibly value-free concepts of legal science; and (4) the division of jurisdiction between ordinary courts and administrative courts. Meanwhile there have been great changes in government and in economic and social institutions; and consequently a substantial disparity between the bases of legal theory and the facts of contemporary life is now apparent. The distinction is in crisis, and this crisis is the subject of a good deal of lively discussion in European juridical circles. It may be useful to examine briefly some of the reasons.

First, civil lawyers have learned a great deal about the common law. It might have been possible for a parochial Continental jurist of the nineteenth century to believe that the common law was crude and barbarous by comparison with the civil law. But increased cultural interaction between the civil and common law worlds, and in particu-lar the flowering of comparative legal studies on the Continent, have revealed to the civil lawyer that Anglo-American common law is not measurably less sensitive, efficient, or just than his own legal system. He is aware that other Western, democratic, capitalist societies than his own have been able to reach an advanced state of legal development without making a technical distinction between public law and private law. This need not lead him to conclude that his own legal system should discard the dichotomy, but it does suggest that it is not a neces-sary part of every developed legal order.

Second, the Nazi regime in Germany, the Fascist period in Italy, a variety of totalitarian governments in Latin America, and the de-velopment of socialist legality in Cuba, Eastern Europe, and the Soviet

Union in this century have all tended to dispel the comfortable illusion that the traditional civil law conceptions of public law and private law expressed ideologically neutral scientific truth. As civil law Europe became ideologically heterogeneous, familiar legal terms took on unfamiliar meanings. Astute civil lawyers have always been aware that these conceptions had, at bottom, an ideological basis, but the political history of this century has broadened and intensified that awareness. Such terms as public law and private law do not import any given meaning; their meaning is supplied by the culture of a given time and place. This truism has been underlined by both those who attack and those who defend traditional conceptions.

Third, governments have changed; today it is common for the state to become involved in the society and the economy. The individualistic state of the nineteenth century has been replaced by the social state of the twentieth. The expanded role of government has often been viewed as leading to a contraction of the area set off for private autonomy. According to one view, fundamental private law concepts have consequently been modified by the addition of social or public elements; such terms as the "socialization" or "publicization" of private law are frequently encountered in the literature. Modern constitutions, starting with the Weimar Constitution of 1919, explicitly limit private rights in the public interest, producing what civil lawyers commonly refer to as the "social function" of property and other private rights. Although a more traditional doctrinal writer may insist that the legal, as distinguished from the social and economic, content of private rights remains unchanged under the new governments, such a distinction is unconvincing. In fact, the content of private rights has been substantially altered.

Fourth, the involvement of the state in the economic life of the nation has, to a growing extent, been carried on by the direct participation of state entities or state-controlled corporations engaged in commercial or industrial enterprise and using the legal forms of private law. In this way the private law exerts a growing force on public activity carried on not through the traditional medium of the administration but through the conduct of industrial and commercial enterprise by state organs or by companies controlled by the state. This tendency

has been summed up by some administrative law scholars as tending toward a "privatization" of public law, an expansion of the role of private law at the expense of administrative law.

Fifth, this century has seen the growth in importance and legal recognition of so-called "intermediate groups"—associations of persons engaged in concerted activity. The earlier image of a legal universe populated solely by the individual and the state, each with its own clearly defined role, is clearly inadequate. In its place is a much more complicated universe, peopled not only by the individual and the state, but also by a wide variety of organizations such as trade unions, co-operatives, foundations, commercial and industrial companies, consortiums, and religious societies. Many of these—one need only mention political parties, trade unions, and commercial and industrial corporations—exercise great economic and social power, particularly in postwar democratic societies. They constitute a kind of "private" government, which frequently has greater impact on the lives of large numbers of individuals than do formally constituted "public" governments. In so complicated a legal universe, simple dichotomies like public law and private law seem to lose their utility.

Sixth, European and Latin American constitutions have come to be the medium for the statement of fundamental individual rights, including property rights, guarantees of the right to engage in economic activity, and the like. Thus the civil codes have been deprived of their constitutional function. That function has been transferred from the most private of private law to the most public of public law sources. In a sense this might be described as a "deconstitutionalization" or "depublicization" of private law. This development tends to reduce the significance of the public law–private law distinction in the eyes of those who see the distinction primarily as a means of protecting individual rights.

Seventh, rigid constitutions and judicial review of the constitutionality of legislation have been established in Austria, Italy, Germany, and other nations in Europe and Latin America. Special constitutional courts exist in some countries, but in others the ordinary judiciary performs this function. This necessarily reduces the significance of rigorous theories about the separation of powers, and tends to blur the

public law—private law distinction in the minds of those who see a close relation between that distinction and the separation of powers.

Eighth, the substantive differences between public law and private law have been reduced by the action of two separate but related forces. For one, the growth of administrative law has produced progressively greater restrictions on the power of the state to disregard or violate the claims of private persons. Pursuit of the *Rechtstaat*—insistence on the applicability of the rule of law to the state itself—leads ultimately to a homogeneous legal system in which the state is merely one kind, although still a very important kind, of subject of the law. This trend has been reinforced by the efforts of scholars to apply the conceptual structure of traditional legal science, originally developed out of the private law, to public law fields. Together the two trends have produced a strong movement toward "privatization" of public law.

Ninth, the traditional aims and methods of legal science and the general theory of law as taught in the law schools, both largely derived from the work of the Pandectists in the nineteenth century, have come under attack during this century by a small but growing scholarly avant-garde. Others, who see the traditional legal science as valid but spent, seek new directions for the fundamental work of legal scholarship. One result is that the scholar's field of interest has expanded beyond the law itself. He is now concerned about how the law relates to the cultural context from which it draws life, and to the society whose problems it must seek to resolve. Another result is a relaxation of emphasis on the validity and usefulness of conceptual structures and logical-formal thinking. The tendency clearly is toward a more "open" jurisprudence and a less technical methodology. In the course of this development, a primarily methodological emphasis on the public law–private law distinction inevitably loses some of its force.

Finally, civil law nations have seen the growth of fields that defy classification as either public or private law. For example, labor law and agrarian law are a mixture of public and private elements, and are incompatible with the traditional classification. Professorial chairs, courses, and institutes in these fields exist in the universities, and journals devoted to them are regularly published. Their existence tends further to blur the distinction between public and private law.

One can say, then, that a rather drastic reshaping of the traditional conceptions of private and public law is under way in the civil law world. The distinction continues, for the reasons mentioned earlier, to have great practical importance. Even under the impact of the forces tending toward newer definitions, substantial areas remain clear, and the great majority of problems and interests remain easily classifiable into one category or the other. But at the frontier between them there is great flux, and few sophisticated civil lawyers today would attempt any functional definition of private law or public law.

The normative effect of the distinction between public and private law tends to overshadow its descriptive utility, but the distinction does also serve a descriptive function. It serves to sum up a division of labor, a separation of the law into smaller parts to facilitate teaching, scholarship, and discussion. But the normative overtones tend to make the distinction a fairly sharp one, even when used in a descriptive sense. A teacher of private law does not, as a rule, attempt to teach or study the public aspects of his subject. Although he teaches about property, for example, he will not discuss property taxation, regulation of urban land use, or the constitutional protection of property rights. These are all parts of public law, and he leaves them to specialists in that area.

He also tends to make very sharp distinctions, even within private and public law, between procedure and substance and between one substantive field and another. On the whole such distinctions seem to be considerably more emphatic in the civil law world than in the common law world. It is unusual for the scholar to follow a problem where it leads him, regardless of boundaries; and the notion that one should keep within one's own territory has gradually become an important assumption of the doctrine, and hence part of the law itself. Indeed, in extreme cases, distinctions of this sort are conceived of as embodying reality, as indicating a classification that is not merely conventional but is based on the nature of the material itself. Hence one occasionally finds doctrinal discussion about the autonomy of certain subjects, even where the field under discussion would seem to have been the result more of historical accident than of any inherent qualities. In an aggravated case a writer may insist that only one of various proposed arrangements of the law is correct.

The civil lawyer thus divides the law into public and private law and a group of hybrids (such as labor law and agrarian law) that have elements of both. Public law itself is further divided into constitutional law, administrative law, and criminal law. Criminal procedure is generally similarly classified, in part because of its close relation to criminal law. The proper classification of civil procedure has been the subject of considerable scholarly discussion. At present, the dominant view favors considering it as part of public law.

Private law is composed of civil law and commercial law. Of these, civil law is much the more important. It is the modern manifestation of the oldest component of the civil law tradition: Roman civil law. Until the general decline of the temporal jurisdiction of ecclesiastical tribunals set in, the civil law lived in a state of symbiosis with the canon law. When systems of justice were secularized, following the Reformation, the civil law survived, greatly enriched by canon law, and the latter lost most of its temporal significance. Today there is a comparable trend toward the absorption of commercial law by civil law.

Commercial law, it will be recalled from Chapter I, began as a separate system of justice created by merchants to govern their own affairs. It had its own rules and customs, its own system of tribunals and judges, its own procedures for adjudication and enforcement, and its own constituency. It was not a part of the official systems of civil, criminal, or ecclesiastical justice. These independent features of commercial law have gradually been lost. Commercial justice was nationalized with the rise of the nation-state. The law of civil procedure was extended to proceedings in commercial courts. Gradually the notion of a separate commercial jurisdiction began to disappear. Today, in some nations, separate commercial courts no longer exist, even in name. In others they have a nominal separate existence at the trial level, but are distinguishable from ordinary civil courts only by the presence of a merchant who sits on the bench together with the civil judges. At the appellate level no distinction exists: the same court that decides civil appeals hears and decides commercial appeals. The commercial court in such a system is no longer a separate court; it is a special sub-jurisdiction of the civil court.

The commercial law continues to be the object of a separate commercial code in most civil law nations. This, however, is also passing. Both Switzerland and Italy have abolished their separate commercial codes, and have combined the matters previously included in them with their civil codes. Those charged with a revision of the French Civil Code have recommended that France take a similar course. Others will surely follow.

Separate chairs in commercial law continue to exist in the universities, and the law libraries of the civil law world contain a substantial literature on commercial law. More and more, however, the trend is toward dominance by the civil lawyers. They are the ones who do the basic theoretical work for the whole of private law (and much of public law). Commercial law doctrine accepts the work of the civil law jurists and builds on it. By a gradual but apparently inexorable process, commercial law has become less a parallel field within the private law area and more a division of, or specialization within, civil law. Civil law is becoming synonymous with private law; commercial law is being "civilized."

As civil law takes over, and as commercial law gradually loses its separate identity, a process analogous to the enrichment of civil law by canon law is taking place. As a general proposition, the civil law has traditionally viewed transactions between individuals as isolated juridical events. The commercial law, by way of contrast, has viewed transactions involving merchants as a part of the normal flow of commerical activity. The difference in attitude has, through the centuries, produced differences in rules and practices. Not surprisingly, the tendency in modern industrial-commercial nations has been to favor the commercial law approach over that of the civil law. This process, predictably, has been described as the "commercialization" of private law.

Private law thus consists of two major fields existing in symbiosis with each other. Civil law is enriched by "commercialization"; commercial law is diminished by "civilization," and is in decline. The tendency is toward a unified private law that is synonymous with civil law. The oldest subtradition in the civil law tradition lives on.

# XV

## THE LEGAL PROFESSIONS

Like the divisions of jurisdiction and of law, described in Chapters XIII and XIV, the division of labor among professional lawyers in the civil law world displays characteristics unfamiliar to the common law world, and particularly to those in the United States. Americans usually think of *the* legal profession, of a single entity. To Americans a lawyer, no matter what kind of legal work he happens to be doing at the moment, is still a lawyer. Although many young graduates start out as private attorneys, government lawyers, or members of the legal staffs of corporations, and stay in those positions for life, it is common for them to change from one branch of the profession to another. During his lifetime a lawyer may do a variety of legal jobs. He may spend a year or so as law clerk to a state or federal judge after graduation from law school. He may spend some time in the office of a district attorney or a city attorney, or in the legal office of a state or federal agency; or he may join a corporate law department. He may then move to private practice. If he has a successful career, he may ultimately secure an appointment as a state or federal judge. Americans think it normal for him to move easily from one position to another, and they do not think it necessary for him to have special training for any of these different kinds of work.

Things are different in civil law jurisdictions. There, a choice among a variety of distinct professional careers faces the young law graduate. He can embark on a career as a judge, a public prosecutor, a government lawyer, an advocate, or a notary. He must make this decision early and then live with it Although it is theoretically possible to move from one of these professions to another, such moves are comparatively rare. The initial choice, once made, tends to be final in the majority of cases. The point of entry into any of these careers is almost always at the bottom, and advancement is frequently as much a function of seniority within the given career as it is of merit. Accumulated ex-

perience in another legal career does not give one a head start or any formal advantage in the process of advancement. Consequently the average young lawyer soon finds himself locked into a career from which escape is likely to be too costly to contemplate.

One predictable result is a tendency for the lines that divide one career from another to sharpen. Those involved in a particular branch of the legal profession come to think of themselves as different from the others. They develop their own expertise, their own career image, their own professional association. Rivalries, jurisdictional problems, and failures of communication between different kinds of lawyers are more likely to occur than they are in the United States, with its single, unified legal profession. England, with its division of the profession into barristers and solicitors, stands a step closer to the civil law model, but still is far from exhibiting the degree of compartmentalization and immobility one generally encounters in the civil law world. Bureaucratization, especially evident in the various governmental legal careers, is measurably greater than in the common law world, where easy lateral mobility among the different branches of the legal profession leads to a quite different mode of entry into and advancement within them.

The tendency of the initial choice of legal career to be final and the resulting sharp separation of each branch of the legal profession from the others combine to produce a number of effects considered undesirable by many civil lawyers. Frequently the career decision is made without an adequate basis for choice, before the young lawyer has been sufficiently exposed to the range of possible legal careers to decide wisely which is the best for him. And the isolation of those in one career from the others, the tendency to identify with only one set of professional interests and functions, encourages a limiting narrowness of attitude and a Balkanization of the legal professions. These are among the reasons why, in certain nations, law graduates are required to undergo a period of practical training, in which they must participate for designated periods in the work of the judiciary, of government lawyers, and of private practice before they can be admitted to any legal career. This institution is most fully developed in Germany, where the law graduate has to spend two-and-one-half years

(called the *Referendarzeit*) in a practical training program following his university legal education.

The judiciary provides an obvious and interesting example of the phenomena we are describing. On graduation from law school (or following the period of practical training, where required) the student who wishes to become a judge immediately applies for admission to the judiciary; if selected (often on the basis of a competitive examination), he enters at the bottom of the profession. Typically he may find himself assigned to the lowest in the hierarchy of courts in a remote part of the country. As the result of some combination of seniority and demonstrated merit, he will gradually rise in the judicial hierarchy to more desirable and prestigious judicial positions, and eventually retire. Normally he will compete for desirable positions only against other members of the judiciary. Although appointment to positions on the highest court—a supreme court of cassation or its equivalent—may in theory be open to distinguished practicing lawyers or professors, such appointments are rare. The highest courts, like the lower courts, are likely to be manned exclusively by those who have risen within the judicial career service. The typical judge will never have practiced law or have served in any other branch of the legal profession, except possibly during required practical training following graduation from the university. He will tend to restrict his professional and social contacts to other judges. He will see the law solely from the judge's point of view. He will be a specialist.

The public prosecutor is also a civil servant, and, typically, he has two principal functions. The first is to act as prosecutor in criminal actions, preparing and presenting the state's cases against the accused before a court. In this sense the public prosecutor is not unlike a district attorney in a typical American state. His second principal function, however, is quite different; he is called on to represent the public interest in judicial proceedings between private individuals. Thus he may have the power to intervene, even at the trial level, in a variety of actions of the sort ordinarily considered to be private matters, involving only the interests of the parties. He may also be required by law to intervene in other matters at the trial level, typically actions involving personal status and family relationships. Finally, in some na-

tions, he may be required to appear and to present his own independent view of the proper interpretation and application of the law in actions before the highest ordinary courts. The theory is that a primary function of such courts is the correct interpretation and application of the law, that parties to cases cannot always be expected to present all the arguments, and that the judge needs the assistance of a public prosecutor to assure that an impartial view, in the interest of the law, is presented.

The young university law graduate who wishes to become a public prosecutor ordinarily takes the state examination for this career shortly after he leaves the university or completes his practical training; if successful, he enters at the bottom of the service and begins a lifetime career in it. Recently there has been a tendency in civil law jurisdictions toward "judicialization" of the public prosecutor service, the idea being that since prosecutors perform quasi-judicial functions, they ought to have something of the independence and security of tenure that is given judges. This trend has reached an advanced stage in several nations, most prominently Italy, where the office of public prosecutor has been made a part of the judiciary. However, the career of judge and that of public prosecutor continue even in these nations to be separate careers within the judiciary; although the trend ultimately may be toward a merger of the two functions, this has not yet taken place. In particular, the relationship between the public prosecutor and the ministry of justice, which exercises authority over his work, continues to be quite different from the relationship of the judge to that ministry. Judicialization of the office of public prosecutor has, however, tended to encourage mobility between the judicial and prosecutorial professions.

In some civil law jurisdictions there is no general career of government lawyer; individual government offices and agencies have their own legal staffs, but appointment, advancement, salary, working conditions, and benefits may vary widely from one agency to another. The lawyer works for a given agency or office, and identifies with it rather than, more generally, with a corps of government lawyers. In other countries, there is an office of government attorneys that provides legal services for all state agencies. Even in the former case, appointment and advancement are bureaucratized and regularized. And

in either case the difficulty of lateral movement to another branch of the profession tends to fix the government lawyer in his career. As with the judicial service and the public prosecutor service, the student who wishes to become a government lawyer takes the state examination after he completes his legal education and practical training, and enters that service at the bottom. Normally he stays with it for life.

The advocate is the closest thing one finds in the civil law to the attorney-at-law in the United States. He meets with and advises clients, and represents them in court. He may also become involved in helping them plan their business and property affairs. He will be a product of a university law school and, typically, of a period of apprenticeship in the office of an experienced lawyer. He will normally practice in a law office in which he is the only senior lawyer, with one or two junior attorneys associated with him. Although law firms resembling those in the United States are beginning to appear more often in certain parts of the civil world, the general rule still is that of the individual law office; indeed, in some countries partnerships for the practice of law are forbidden. Frequently there are similar restrictions on the development of corporate law departments or similar "house counsel" arrangements. This kind of restriction is the product of a traditional ideal of the lawyer as a totally independent person who is free to accept or reject clients, and who makes his own decisions about how the client's affairs should be handled. However, there is a growing trend toward evasion of such restrictions, so it is not uncommon to find groups of lawyers practicing together in what look like partnerships or corporate law departments in a jurisdiction in which such arrangements appear to be forbidden by statute or by regulation of the bar association. Generally all practicing advocates must be members of a bar association, which frequently is officially recognized and has the authority to establish rules governing the practice of the profession, including fee schedules. As in the United States and elsewhere, members of the practicing bar are likely to become involved in politics and to move into high public office. Although the matter varies from nation to nation, in many civil law countries the percentage of high public officials who began their careers as practicing lawyers is as high or higher than is the case in the United States.

If the civil law advocate closely resembles our practicing lawyer,

any similarity between the civil law notary and the notary public in common law countries is only superficial. The historical origins of the civil law notary and the common law notary public are the same, but the two occupations have developed along very different lines. Our notary public is a person of very slight importance. The civil law notary is a person of considerable importance. The notary in the typical civil law country serves three principal functions. First, he drafts important legal instruments, such as wills, corporate charters, conveyances, and contracts. Although advocates sometimes get involved in drafting instruments, the notary continues to do most of this work in civil law nations. (In spite of the notary's established position in this field, however, there is some tension between advocates and notaries over jurisdictional matters.) Second, the notary authenticates instruments. An authenticated instrument (called everywhere in the civil law world a "public act") has special evidentiary effects: it conclusively establishes that the instrument itself is genuine, and that what it recites accurately represents what the parties said and what the notary saw and heard. Evidence that contradicts the statements in a public act is not admissible in an ordinary judicial proceeding. One who wishes to attack the authenticity of a public act must institute a special action for the purpose, and such an action is rarely brought. Third, the notary acts as a kind of public record office. He is required to retain a copy of every instrument he prepares and furnish authenticated copies on request. An authenticated copy usually has the same evidentiary value as an original.

Notaries are usually given quasi-monopolies. A typical civil law nation will be divided into notarial districts, and in each district a limited number of notaries will have exclusive competence. Unlike advocates, who are free to refuse to serve a client, the notary must serve all comers. This, added to his functions as record office and his monopoly position, tends to make him a public as well as private functionary. Access to the profession of notary is difficult because the number of notarial offices is quite limited. Candidates for notarial positions must ordinarily be graduates of university law schools, and must serve an apprenticeship in a notary's office. Typically, aspirants for such positions will take a national examination, and if successful,

will be appointed to a vacancy when it occurs. Ordinarily there will be a national notaries organization that will serve the same sort of functions for notaries as the national bar association serves for advocates and other organizations for judges, prosecutors, and government lawyers.

We come finally to the academic lawyer, who teaches in the law schools and writes the doctrine that, as was explained in Chapter IX, strongly influences all aspects of the legal process in the civil law tradition. He is the inheritor of the tradition of the Roman jurisconsult and of the medieval scholar, whose opinions, at some periods in the history of the civil law tradition, have had formal authority to bind judges. Formal authority aside, the academic lawyer is generally viewed as the person who does the fundamental thinking for the entire legal profession. His ideas, as expressed in books and articles, and his opinions on specific legal questions raised in litigation or lawmaking, particularly in the areas covered by the basic codes, are of substantially greater importance than the work of academic lawyers in the common law world.

It is not easy to become a professor in a civil law university. The road to appointment to a vacant chair is long, arduous, and full of hazards. The young aspirant to an academic career attaches himself to a professor as an assistant, sometimes with pay and sometimes without. Eventually, after meeting certain more or less formal requirements and publishing a book, he will be examined for admission to the category of "private-docent." If he receives this title, he is considered to be qualified for an academic post. When a chair becomes vacant, he will compete for it against other private-docents and, if the post is a desirable one, against professors who hold less prestigious chairs. Throughout this process his progress may depend as much on the influence of the professor to whom he has attached himself as on his demonstrated ability as a scholar. This system gives the professor great power over those who have attached themselves to him, and makes them heavily dependent on him for their careers. The result is an academic world composed of professors surrounded by retinues of assistants. These assistants are expected to think and work along the same lines as the professor, and thus "schools of thought" are established and grow.

Doctrinal, as well as personal, loyalty is expected by the professor, whose power over the assistant's career enables him to demand it.

The uncertainty of success in pursuit of a professorship is so great that few can afford to gamble exclusively on it. In addition, in many civil law nations professors are not expected to spend all, or even a major portion, of their time at the law school. In Latin America, in particular, their rates of compensation reflect this assumption; they are by any standard extremely low. The formal obligations of the professor are to lecture to his classes a few hours a week and to give examinations (with the help of his assistants) two or three times a year. He is not paid enough for this to live well, and he consequently divides most of his time between another legal career—usually in practice, in the judiciary, or in public office—and his own and his assistants' doctrinal writing. While professors are full-time teacher-scholars in some parts of the civil law world, such as Germany, these are exceptions to the general rule. The trend is in the direction of full time, but it is still only a trend.

Thus an aspirant to an academic position customarily embarks on an additional legal career, both as a hedge against possible failure in the academic world and as an additional source of income, even if he is successful in the competition for a chair. The professor is not full-time and is not expected to be. In the usual case he is also a practicing lawyer, and the prestige of his title as professor may be of most importance to him because of the business it will bring to his law office. An advocate with the title of professor will attract important clients and will be called upon to prepare opinions on legal questions by other lawyers (and also by judges) and be paid for them.

The tendency of the law professor also to be a practicing lawyer produces what appears to common lawyers to be a curious sort of professional schizophrenia. As a lawyer, he will be pragmatic, concrete, and result-oriented. He will follow the problem where it leads him, regardless of boundaries between fields of the law. He will be fact-conscious. He will seek and cite judicial decisions. He will be a tough, partisan advocate. As a professor, he will write and teach in the prevailing doctrinal style, working in the central tradition of legal science. Both his writing and his teaching will prominently display the aca-

demic characteristics typical of legal scholarship in the civil law world, and he may even exaggerate such characteristics to overcompensate because he is also a practicing lawyer. He becomes aggressively academic, as a kind of reaction against his practical work as advocate. His life is divided into two separate halves, and he adopts a different professional personality for each.

These, then, are the principal actors in the legal process in the civil law tradition: the judge, the prosecuting attorney, the government lawyer, the advocate, the notary, and the law professor–scholar. Each is a specialist. The legal profession is a fragmented one, in contrast with the more strongly unified legal profession in common law nations. The difference is an important one; it both reflects and reinforces more fundamental differences between the two legal traditions. These differences can be illustrated by briefly reconsidering the differences between the civil law judge and the common law judge.

We have seen in earlier chapters that the civil law judge is relegated to a comparatively minor role in the legal process. His work is, in a sense, routine work. He does not create and formulate policy; he applies rules created and formulated by others, according to procedures they dictate. Consequently the approach to judicial organization, although it has its own special characteristics, is similar in many ways to the organization of other kinds of civil service. Young people enter at the bottom and advance according to seniority and merit. There are regular procedures for advancement and for periodic evaluations of performance. Since judicial work is viewed as routine and uncreative, it can safely be put into the hands of young, inexperienced people. Such people, it is true, get minor judicial posts early in their careers, progressing to more important matters as they acquire experience. But it is *judicial* experience that qualifies them to handle the more important work. Experience in other branches of the legal profession does not count.

The prevailing image of the judge tends to become self-justifying. The career is attractive to those who lack ambition, who seek security, and who are unlikely to be successful as practicing lawyers or in the competition for an academic post. Working conditions and rates of

pay conform to this image. The better law graduate accordingly looks elsewhere for his career. The result is that in some parts of the civil law world the judicial career has become a haven for second-raters. Even in such nations there are, of course, some excellent judges, but the average quality is likely to be low. The best legal minds are usually found elsewhere, particularly in practice and in academic life. The legal profession has a clearly defined class structure; judges are the lower class.

The quality and the status of judges thus become a fairly reliable index of the continuing strength, within a given nation, of the image of the legal process that grew out of the legal revolution and was strengthened and refined by legal science. Where, as in much of Latin America, the grip of these traditions is very strong, the quality and status of the judiciary are low. This effect is reinforced (and complicated) by the additional factor of social class-consciousness. The upper classes, who get the best education and who have influential friends, tend to have privileged access to and to dominate practice and academic life. Judicial posts are frequently filled by those who are rising to the middle class from humbler social origins. In this way the judicial career provides a convenient avenue of social mobility.

But where, as in several European nations, the extremes of the revolutionary model of the legal process have lost much of their power and the grip of legal science on the legal mind is loosening, there is a perceptible tendency toward a judiciary of higher quality and status. It is true that this tendency is strongest outside the ordinary judiciary. The most prominent examples are constitutional courts of the kind recently created in Austria, Germany, and Italy (described in Chapter XVIII) and administrative courts like the judicial section of the French Council of State. But even within the ordinary judiciary, the powers—and hence the status—of the judge have been increasing. The achievement of the French judiciary in creating and developing law where the Code Napoléon was silent or inadequate is well-known. The power of ordinary Italian judges to give a preliminary decision on whether a constitutional objection raised in a civil or criminal proceeding is "manifestly unfounded" is another example. Growing judicial awareness of the close relation between a decision interpreting a statute

and the probable result of a constitutional attack on that statute is yet another. Such changes, combined with a growing realistic concern about the inadequacy of the traditional model of the judicial process, are most strongly felt in the historically more important civil law nations: France, Germany, and Italy. Although it is unlikely that anything like the common law judge will emerge from this evolution, it does seem probable that the status of the "judicial class" within the legal profession will increase. This, in turn, may tend to reduce the sharpness of the separation between judges and other kinds of lawyers.

# XVI

## CIVIL PROCEDURE

JUST AS CIVIL LAW is the heart of the substantive law in the civil law tradition, so civil procedure is the heart of procedural law. Strictly speaking, the law of civil procedure applies only to the process of judicial enforcement of rights and duties arising under the civil law part of private law. The distinct nature and purposes of criminal proceedings and the existence of separate sets of courts, such as administrative courts, have produced separate bodies of criminal procedure and administrative procedure. But all systems of procedure in the civil law tradition have a common origin in Roman, canon, and medieval Italic law. All have tended to follow the lead of civil proceduralists in molding and developing procedural law. Civil procedure is central and basic, and special procedural systems—even criminal procedure—have tended to develop as variations on the civil procedure model.

At the same time, there are important differences between civil and criminal proceedings, and criminal procedure has, particularly since the period of revolutions, been an essentially independent field of regulation and study. Most civil law systems include separate codes of civil procedure and criminal procedure. The subjects are separately taught in the law schools, and a separate literature has grown up around each of them. At a very fundamental level, however, they are based on common notions, and the development of such notions—general theories and general principles of procedure—is traditionally assumed to be the job of the civil proceduralist, just as the development of general theories and principles of law, as shown in the preceding chapter, is primarily the task of the civil lawyer.

A typical civil proceeding in a civil law jurisdiction is divided into separate stages. In Italy, for example, there is a preliminary stage, in which the pleadings are submitted and a hearing judge appointed; the evidence-taking stage, in which the hearing judge takes the evidence, and prepares a summary written record; and a decisional stage,

in which the judges who will decide the case consider the record, receive counsel's briefs, hear their arguments, and render decisions. The reader will observe that the word "trial" is missing from this description. In a very general way it can be said that what common lawyers think of as a trial in civil proceedings does not exist in the civil law world. The reason is that the right to a jury in civil actions, traditional in the common law world, has never taken hold in the civil law world. This tradition continues most strongly in the United States today, where in most jurisdictions there is a constitutional right to a civil jury.

The existence of a jury has profoundly affected the form of civil proceedings in the common law tradition. The necessity to bring together a number of ordinary citizens to hear the testimony of witnesses and observe the evidence, to find the facts, and to apply the facts to the law under instructions from a judge, has pushed the trial into the shape of an event. The lay jury cannot easily be convened, adjourned, and reconvened several times in the course of a single action without causing a great deal of inconvenience and expense. It seems much more natural and efficient for the parties, their counsel, the judge, and the jury to be brought together at a certain time and place in order to perform, once and for all, that part of the civil proceeding that requires their joint participation. Such an event is a trial as we know it.

In the civil law nations, where there is no tradition of civil trial by jury, an entirely different approach has developed. There is no such thing as a trial in our sense; there is no single, concentrated event. The typical civil proceeding in a civil law country is actually a series of isolated meetings of and written communications between counsel and the judge, in which evidence is introduced, testimony is given, procedural motions and rulings are made, and so on. Matters of the sort that would ordinarily be concentrated into a single event in a common law jurisdiction will be spread over a large number of discrete appearances and written acts before the judge who is taking the evidence. Comparative lawyers, in remarking on this phenomenon, speak of the "concentration" of the trial in common law countries and the lack of such concentration in civil law countries. In general it can be said that civil lawyers favor the more concentrated system and that

the trend in civil law jurisdictions has been toward greater concentration, with the rate of development varying widely. (Austria and Germany seem to be moving most rapidly in this direction.) The tradition, however, continues to be one of relative lack of concentration.

Lack of concentration has some interesting secondary consequences. For one thing, pleading is very general, and the issues are defined as the proceeding goes on; this practice differs considerably from that found in common law jurisdictions, where precise formulation of the issues in pleadings and pretrial proceedings is seen as necessary preparation for the concentrated event of the trial. For somewhat similar reasons, the civil law attorney typically spends less time in preparing for an appearance before the court during the evidence-taking part of the civil proceeding. The appearance is usually for the purpose of examining only one witness or of introducing only one or two pieces of material evidence. The pressure to prepare the entire case at the very beginning, felt by the common lawyer preparing for trial, does not exist. The element of surprise is reduced to a minimum, since each appearance is relatively brief and involves a fairly small part of the total case. There will be plenty of time to prepare some sort of response before the next appearance. The lack of concentration also explains the lesser importance of discovery (advance information about the opponent's witnesses and evidence) and pretrial procedures (preliminary discussions with opposing counsel and the judge to reach agreement on matters not really at issue and so on). Discovery is not necessary because there is little, if any, tactical or strategic advantage to be gained from the element of surprise. There is no necessity for pretrial proceedings because there is no trial; in a sense every appearance in the first two stages of a civil law proceeding has both trial and pretrial characteristics.

A second characteristic of the traditional civil law proceeding is that evidence is received and the summary record prepared by someone other than the judge who will decide the case. We have seen in Chapter II that contemporary procedural institutions in the civil law world have been strongly influenced by medieval canonic procedures. In the canon law proceeding, evidence was taken by a clerk, and it was the clerk's written record that the judge used in making his decision. This procedure eventually was modified to place the evidence-taking

part of the proceeding under the guidance of a judge, but quite often the case would still be decided by other judges, or by a panel of judges that included the judge who took the evidence. Comparative lawyers customarily contrast this form of proceeding with the custom in the common law system by which the evidence is heard and seen directly and immediately by the judge who is to decide the case. Accordingly it has become common to speak of the "immediacy" of the common law trial, as distinguished from the "mediacy" of the civil law proceeding. Here again, comparative commentators tend to think of the common law system as preferable, and there is a steady evolution in civil law jurisdictions toward greater immediacy. The "documentary curtain" that separated the judge from the parties during the medieval period and that was then thought to produce a greater likelihood of fair proceedings, unaffected by influence brought to bear on the judges by interested persons, no longer seems necessary. On the contrary, preparation of the record by someone other than the judge who is to decide the case is now seen to be a defect because it deprives the judge of the opportunity to see and hear the parties, to observe their demeanor, and to evaluate their statements directly.

In a mediate system, procedure tends to become primarily a written matter. Those in common law countries think of a trial as an event during which witnesses are sworn and orally examined and cross-examined in the presence of the judge and jury. Motions and objections are often made orally by counsel, and the judge rules orally on them. In the civil law, on the contrary, even the questions asked a witness during the civil proceedings are often asked by the judge on the basis of questions submitted in writing by counsel for the parties. Where the practice persists of having one person receive the evidence and make the record and another decide the case, a written rather than oral proceeding is obviously necessary. A trend toward immediacy in civil proceedings carries with it a trend toward orality, and orality is promoted also by the trend toward concentration. Civil law proceduralists think of the three matters as related to one another, and one frequently encounters discussions in which concentration, immediacy, and orality are advanced as interrelated components of proposals for reform in the law of civil procedure.

Foreign observers are sometimes confused by the fact that, in some

civil law nations, questions are put to witnesses by the judge rather than by counsel for the parties. This leads some to the conclusion that the civil law judge determines what questions to ask and, unlike the common law system, in effect determines the scope and extent of the inquiry. People talk about an "inquisitorial" system of proof-taking, as contrasted with the "adversary" system of the common law. The characterization is quite misleading. In fact, the prevailing system in both the civil law and the common law world is the "dispositive" system, according to which the determination of what issues to raise, what evidence to introduce, and what arguments to make is left almost entirely to the parties. Judges in both traditions have some power to undertake inquiries on their own, but civil law judges seldom exercise this power. The common law judge is more inclined to intervene, but usually does so only when juveniles or other incapacitated persons are involved in a case, or where there appears to be a clear public interest that the parties are not adequately representing. In similar cases in civil law jurisdictions, a public prosecutor or similar official is required by law to participate in the proceeding as a representative of the public interest. But these are exceptional occurances, and in the great mass of civil litigation in both traditions the rule is that the parties have considerable power to determine what will take place in the proceedings. Where the civil law judge puts questions to the witness, he does so at the request of counsel, and he ordinarily limits his questions to those submitted by the lawyers.

The practice of putting the judge between the lawyer and the witness does, however, further illustrate the traditional lack of orality in the civil law. Ordinarily the lawyer who wishes to put questions to a witness must first prepare a written statement of "articles of proof," which describes the matters on which he wishes to question the witness. These articles go to both the judge and the opposing counsel in advance of the hearing at which the witness is to be examined. In this way the opposing counsel (and possibly also the witness himself) has advance written knowledge of what will go on at the hearing and can prepare for it. This profoundly affects the psychological positions of questioning lawyer and responding witness at the hearing, and the fact that any questions the lawyer asks must pass through the judge

at the hearing reinforces this effect. The familiar pattern of immediate, oral, rapid examination and cross-examination of witnesses in a common law trial is not present in the civil law proceeding.

A number of factors explain the substantial differences in the law of evidence between the civil law and the common law tradition. One of the most important of these, again, is the matter of the jury. In civil actions in common law jurisdictions, a variety of exclusionary rules, rules determining the admissibility or inadmissibility of offered evidence, have as their prime historical explanation the desire to prevent the jury from being misled by untrustworthy evidence. An alternative policy, one providing that the common law jury be warned of the unreliability of the evidence but then be allowed to evaluate it on the basis of the warning, has uniformly been rejected. The evidence is totally excluded.

Such rules do not exist in civil law jurisdiction because of the absence of a jury in civil actions. This does not mean, however, that evidence can be freely introduced without restriction in civil law proceedings. On the contrary, there are a number of restricting and excluding devices. However, the origin of, and the functions served by, these rules are different from those of exclusionary rules in the common law. To understand these rules we must first go back to the medieval system of "legal proof."

Introduction of the system of legal proof in judicial proceedings was an important civilizing development in European law. It replaced trial by battle and trial by ordeal, the standard methods of deciding litigation in the turbulent feudal world of early medieval Europe. Even though it seems arbitrary, crude, and unjust to us today, this system of legal proof, when it was introduced, exerted a great humanizing influence on the administration of justice, and was a long step forward in the attempt to turn judicial proceedings into rational investigations of the truth of conflicting allegations. The civil law judge then, as now, was not a very powerful person. However honest he might wish to be, he could not easily withstand persuasion, bribery, or threats—particularly threats made by the wealthy and powerful. To be workable at all, the system of legal proof had to provide some means of protecting judges from such pressures. The means that were

developed included a set of formal rules for weighing testimony, a set of exclusionary rules, and the institution of the decisory oath (i.e. an oath that would decide a fact at issue).

The rules governing the weight to be given to certain kinds of testimony were mechanical in operation. The court was required to give predetermined weight to testimony based on the number, status, age, and sex of the witnesses. To prove a fact, a given number of witnesses was required. The testimony of nobles, clerics, and property owners prevailed over that of commoners, laymen, and those without property. The testimony of an older man prevailed over that of a younger. The testimony of women was either barred or given a fraction of the weight of a man's testimony. These and similar rules for evaluating evidence, in which all evidence was given an *a priori* arithmetical value (full proof, half proof, quarter proof, and the like), were based on what was believed to be common experience.

The exclusionary rules disqualified certain kinds of people from testifying at all. The principal groups of such people were the parties, relatives of the parties, and interested third persons. Their testimony was considered basically untrustworthy, and hence was entirely excluded. Here again, the principal reason was probably to protect the weak judge against force and undue influence, and to protect the corrupt judge against bribery. Rather than leave the judge vulnerable to pressures from interested persons, the law protected him by denying admissibility of any kind to the testimony of such persons.

The decisory oath worked in the following way: Party *A* could put Party *B* on his oath as to a fact at issue that was within Party *B*'s knowledge. If Party *B* refused to swear, the fact was taken as conclusively proved against him. If Party *B* swore, the fact was taken as conclusively proved in his favor. The compulsion on Party *B* against swearing falsely lay not only in the religious consequences of a false oath, but also in his criminal liability for perjury.

The early institution of the civil jury in England inhibited the development of some of these restrictions (and led to others) on the introduction and evaluation of evidence in the common law. A group of laymen was less vulnerable to threats of violence or other forms of influence than was a single judge, particularly if the jurors were the

"peers" of the parties, as the common law required. Consequently the need for protection provided to the civil law judge by the system of formal proof was not so strongly felt. The need to protect the jury against unreliable testimony led not only to the disqualification of interested persons as witnesses, but also to a set of restrictions on the admissibility of certain kinds of testimony by qualified witnesses. The jury as finder of fact fulfilled the function served by the decisory oath in two ways: It was an effective method of fact-finding, and it relieved the vulnerable judge of the dangers of party influence in deciding the facts. In this way, although the institution of the civil jury developed its own formalistic characteristics, the system of formal proof and the decisory oath failed to develop the importance in the common law that they acquired on the Continent.

Traces of these medieval devices still exist in the civil law world. The mechanical rules of legal proof have evolved into the irrebuttable presumptions of modern civil law. In some civil law jurisdictions, parties are still disqualified from testifying. The decisory oath remains in effect today in many countries (among them France, Italy, and Spain), although its use is primarily tactical. In general, however, the movement for procedural reform has had as its objective what is called "free evaluation of the evidence" by the judge. Such a movement was given great impetus by the rationalist spirit of the revolutionary period, but its thrust has been limited by the general weakness of the civil law judge and by the widespread mistrust of judges among civil lawyers. Nevertheless, proceduralists in civil law jurisdictions generally regard free evaluation of the evidence as the ideal toward which reform should point.

As a general rule there is a right to an appeal in civil law jurisdictions. "Appeal" has a special meaning here that is unfamiliar in the United States, where it is thought of as primarily a method of correcting mistakes of law made by the trial court. In the civil law tradition, the right of appeal includes the right to reconsideration of factual, as well as legal issues. Although the tendency commonly is to rely on the record prepared below as the factual basis for reconsideration of the case, in many jurisdictions the parties have the right to introduce new evidence at the appellate level. The appellate bench is

expected to consider all of the evidence itself and to arrive at an independent determination of what the facts are and what their significance is. It is also required to prepare its own fully reasoned opinion, in which it discusses both factual and legal issues.

In addition to the technical appeal, the dissatisfied party typically has the right to a further hearing before a higher court. In some jurisdictions (e.g. France and Italy) this procedure is called recourse in cassation; in others (e.g. Germany) it is called revision. The function, in either case, is similar: to provide an authoritative, final determination of any questions of law involved in the case. Recourse in cassation and revision, in other words, approximate the typical functions of common law appellate courts, which ordinarily restrict their consideration on appeal to questions of law. Recourse in cassation and revision have a somewhat different flavor, however, because of the historical background out of which the courts that employ them have developed.

It will be recalled from the discussion in Chapter VII that the extremes of the revolutionary ideology denied any interpretative function to the courts, and that the Tribunal of Cassation was established in France as a nonjudicial tribunal, to which questions of interpretation of the law would be referred by the courts in order to relieve the legislature of the burden of supplying authoritative legislative interpretations. Over the years, the Tribunal of Cassation has become a recognized court, not only in France, but in all jurisdictions following the French model. In these jurisdictions the supreme court of cassation is the highest ordinary court, and it has the function of insuring the correct observance and uniform interpretation of the law. By a somewhat different but analogous process, the institution of revision was developed in Germany, Austria, and Switzerland. Although there are many important differences between revision and recourse in cassation, these institutions serve similar functions. A high court at the apex of the ordinary judiciary has the power to review decisions of the lower courts to determine whether they have correctly interpreted and applied the law. As in the French case, the Austrian, German, and Swiss courts are also responsible for ensuring the uniform interpretation of the law; consequently, although in theory their decisions

are not binding on themselves or on lower courts, theirs is the final voice on the meaning to be given to provisions of law throughout the ordinary courts.

Thus a litigant in a civil law jurisdiction has somewhat broader powers of *direct attack* on a judgment than does a litigant in the common law jurisdictions: he is entitled to an appeal in which he may introduce new evidence in support of his case and in which he is entitled to a new consideration of the facts as well as the law. He may also be entitled to recourse in cassation or revision on questions of law. At the same time, he has a substantially narrower possibility of making an effective *collateral attack* on a judgment than is the case in the common law tradition. (A collateral attack is an objection to the enforcement of a judgment that has become final either because all avenues of appeal have been exhausted or because the opportunity to appeal has been lost through lapse of time.) Basically the matter is one of relative formalism, and we here see a case in which the common law is the more formalistic system. In the common law world, and particularly in the United States, certain types of technical procedural defects, even though basically harmless and easily curable in the ordinary course of the proceedings, can be raised effectively as defenses against the enforcement of a final judgment. The civil law attitude is, in general, that attacks on judgments should be restricted as much as possible to direct attacks, with collateral attacks limited to those instances in which it clearly appears that the procedural defects were of the sort that could not be adequately corrected in the course of the proceeding itself. Hence, for example, improper service of process is valid if it achieves its purpose of notifying the defendant of the action. Many procedural defects can be complained of by a party only within a very brief period after the defective act occurred or after knowledge of the defective act came to the party's notice. In this way defects not raised quickly are cured.

In general, there are no separate concurring or dissenting opinions, even at the appellate level, in civil law jurisdictions. Although exceptions do exist, the general rule is one of unanimity and anonymity. Even dissenting votes are not noted, and it is considered unethical for a judge to indicate that he has taken a position at variance with that an-

nounced in the decision of the court. A recent tendency toward noting dissents and separate concurrences, and even toward the publication of separate opinions, has developed in the constitutional courts of some civil law jurisdictions. But the standard attitude is that the law is certain and should appear so, and that this certainty would be impaired by noting dissents and by publishing separate opinions.

Another fundamental difference between the civil law and common law traditions occurs in enforcement proceedings. Civil law jurisdictions have nothing comparable to the common law notion of civil contempt of court. In Chapter VIII we noted that in the common law a person can be compelled to act or to refrain from acting by the threat of imprisonment or fine for contempt of court—that is, for refusing to obey a court order addressed to him as a person. There is, it is commonly said, a wide range of effective action *in personam* in the common law. The civil law, by way of contrast, knows no civil contempt of court and tends to operate solely *in rem*. This means that regardless of the type of claim one has against another person, the only way one can collect the claim is by obtaining a money judgment against him. The reverberations of this difference reach well back into the legal process, affecting, for example, the very legal definition of a contract. According to the civil law tradition, a promise that cannot be converted into money does not create a legal obligation; if the promise is not enforceable in money terms, it is not enforceable at all. The lack of a power to act *in personam* also affects every aspect of the civil proceeding in the civil law tradition. The power to compel the production of documents, business records, and other evidence or to subject a party or his property to inspection is much weaker than it is in common law jurisdictions. Judicial remedies in civil proceedings are restricted almost entirely to remedies that can be enforced against the property of the defendant (e.g. attachment and sale of his property, delivery of specific property to the claimant, or eviction from the property) or acts that can be performed by a third person and charged to the defendant (e.g. destruction of a structure unlawfully built).

If one stands back and looks at the two systems of civil procedure, the outlines of two somewhat different ideologies begin to emerge. In the common law world the judge is an authority figure who adminis-

ters a merged system of law and of equity. (It must be remembered that the court of equity originated as a court of conscience.) Actions are traditionally tried in the presence of a jury composed of a group of neighbors of the plaintiff and defendant who bring to bear throughout the proceeding the prevailing attitudes and values of the community. The judge has a civil contempt power, enabling him to order people to act or refrain from acting and to punish them if they refuse. The whole proceeding is permeated by a moralistic flavor. The parties play out their roles before the father-judge and the neighbor-jury. In the civil law tradition, by way of contrast, a judge is an important public servant, but he lacks anything like the measure of authority and paternal character possessed by the common law judge. Parties and witnesses can disobey his orders with less fear of serious reprisal. There is no jury of neighbors to look on, approving or disapproving. The civil law tradition is more thoroughly secularized, less moralistic, and more immune to the ethic of the time and place.

This basic difference in general outlook is dramatically illustrated by the law of damages. In the common law world we see nothing extraordinary in the awarding of penal damages, multiple damages, and so-called general damages (that is, damages over and above those proved) in civil actions against defendants whose conduct appears to be malicious or grossly negligent. In the civil law tradition, however, such damages are rarely available to a plaintiff in a civil proceeding. The line between the civil and the criminal is more sharply drawn, and morally reprehensible (i.e. malicious or grossly negligent) actions are matters for the criminal law rather than for the civil law. In the civil trial, as a general rule, the plaintiff's recovery is limited to compensation for the loss he suffered. If the judgment of the community is going to be brought to bear on a defendant because of the moral character of his action, it must be done through the processes of the criminal law, where the defendant is protected from arbitrary or exaggerated imposition of penalties by the principle of the criminal law that no penalty be assessed for something that was not legally defined as a crime at the time the action took place. And, as is generally true of criminal law in Western nations, the penalties in such cases are limited to those established in the statute.

# XVII

## CRIMINAL PROCEDURE

ALTHOUGH THE revolution profoundly affected every part of the civil law tradition, its effects are most clearly observable in public law. And, within the field of public law, much of the criticism of the *ancien régime* and much of the call for reform tended to be concentrated in the field of criminal procedure. Among the writers and philosophers of the eighteenth century who contributed to the ideology of revolution, most had something to say about the sorry state of criminal law and criminal procedure. The most important commentator in this field was Cesare Beccaria, whose book *Of Crimes and Punishments* exploded on the European scene in 1764, and has since become the most influential work on criminal procedure in Western history.

Substantive criminal law in Western, capitalist civil law countries does not differ greatly from that of common law countries. The same kinds of actions are considered criminal, and the same general approaches to punishment are discussed and debated throughout Western culture. There are, however, significant operational differences in criminal procedure, and it is striking to observe the extent to which the revolutionary reform of criminal procedure reflects the causes and effects of the revolutionary period in the civil law tradition. We can illustrate this point by examining the principal thesis and the organization of Beccaria's book.

He begins by establishing the principle of *nullum crimen sine lege* and *nulla poena sine lege*. As Beccaria states it: "Only the laws can determine the punishment of crimes; and the authority of making penal laws can reside only with the legislator, who represents the whole society united by the social compact." Thus, according to Beccaria, crimes and punishments can be established only by law, and by law he means statute. Beccaria then proceeds to discuss the interpretation of laws. His position is that "judges in criminal cases have no

right to interpret the penal laws, because they are not legislators." And further, "the disorders that may arise from a rigorous observance of the letter of penal laws are not to be compared to those produced by the interpretation of them. ... When the code of laws is once fixed, it should be observed in the literal sense, and nothing more is left to the judge than to determine whether an action be or be not conformable to the written law." In the same paragraph, speaking of judges, he refers to "the despotism of this multitude of tyrants." Later, in the chapter on obscurity in the law, he says: "If the power of interpreting laws be an evil, obscurity in them must be another, as the former is the consequence of the latter. This evil will be still greater if the laws be written in a language unknown to the people; who, being ignorant of the consequences of their own actions, become necessarily dependent on a few, who are interpreters of the laws, which, instead of being public and general, are thus rendered private and particular." Beccaria then goes on to establish two basic principles. The first is that there should be a proportion between crimes and punishments, so that the more serious crimes are more severely punished. The second is that punishments should apply impartially to criminals, regardless of their social station, position, or wealth.

The reader will observe the similarity of these observations to the general characteristics of the revolutionary legal tradition, described in Chapter III. They are permeated with state positivism, rationalism, and a concern for the rights of man as enunciated by the school of secular natural law. Principles similar to those stated by Beccaria were, at the same time, affecting the evolution of criminal procedure in the common law world. One difference, however, was the emphasis on, perhaps the exaggeration of, these principles in Europe as a result of the French Revolution and the effect of that revolution on the thinking about law and the state in the civil law world. Hence even today one finds a sharper emphasis in civil law jurisdictions on the principle that every crime and every penalty shall be embodied in a statute enacted by the legislature. To a civil lawyer, common law courts seem to violate this principle every day when they award penal damages, multiple damages, or general damages in civil actions, when they convict people of "common law" crimes, and when they sum-

marily punish people for contempt. Another significant difference between the two traditions is the earlier movement toward reform of penology in the civil law world. Under the influence of Beccaria and his successors, the death penalty was abolished in Tuscany in the eighteenth century, and fundamental reforms leading to less drastic penalties for minor offenses took place throughout Europe well in advance of such reforms in Great Britain and the United States.

It is obvious that an emphasis on the principle of legality (no crime or penalty without a statute enacted by the legislature), together with a desire to have such statutes written down as part of a rational scheme in a language that could be read by the citizen, should lead to codification of the criminal law. In fact, the first object of codification in revolutionary France was the criminal law, and a criminal code was actually written during the Revolution. If a case for codification exists, it exists most clearly in the fields of criminal law and procedure. But once the case is made for criminal law, it is easily extended to other fields, particularly in a legal tradition in which judges are distrusted and a representative legislature is a hero. This, as we have seen, was the case throughout the revolutionary period in the civil law world.

One of the commonest comparisons one hears made about criminal procedure in the two traditions is that the criminal procedure in the civil law tradition is "inquisitorial," while that in the common law tradition is "accusatorial." Although this generalization is inaccurate and misleading as applied to contemporary systems of criminal procedure, it has some validity when put into historical context. In a sense it can be said that the evolution of criminal procedure in the last two centuries in the civil law world has been away from the extremes and abuses of the inquisitorial system, and that the evolution in the common law world during the same period has been away from the abuses and excesses of the accusatorial system. The two systems, in other words, are converging from different directions toward roughly equivalent mixed systems of criminal procedure.

Let us first consider the accusatorial system, which is generally thought by anthropologists to be the first substitute an evolving society develops for private vengeance. In such a system the power to institute the action resides in the wronged person, who is the accuser.

This same right of accusation is soon extended to his relatives, and as the conception of social solidarity and the need for group protection develops, the right of accusation extends to all members of the group. A presiding officer is selected to hear the evidence, decide, and sentence; he does not, however, have the power to institute the action or to determine the questions to be raised or the evidence to be introduced, and he has no inherent investigative powers. These matters are in the hands of the accuser and the accused. The criminal trial is a contest between the accuser and the accused, with the judge as a referee. Typically the proceeding takes place publicly and orally, and is not preceded by any official (i.e. judicial or police) investigation or preparation of evidence.

The inquisitorial system typically represents an additional step along the path of social evolution from the system of private vengeance. Its principle features include first, attenuation or elimination of the figure of the private accuser and appropriation of that role by public officials; and second, the conversion of the judge from an impartial referee into an active inquisitor who is free to seek evidence and to control the nature and objectives of the inquiry. In addition, the relative equality of the parties that is an attribute of the accusatorial system, in which two individuals contest before an impartial arbiter, has been drastically altered. Now the contest is between an individual (the accused) and the state. Historically, inquisitorial proceedings have tended to be secret and written rather than public and oral. The resulting imbalance of power, combined with the secrecy of the written procedure, creates the danger of an oppressive system, in which the rights of the accused can easily be abused. The most infamous analogue familiar to us in the common law world is the Star Chamber, which was basically an inquisitorial tribunal.

The Star Chamber was, however, exceptional in the common law tradition. Historically the system was basically accusatorial in nature, and the early development of the jury as a necessary participant in the criminal proceeding in England tended to prevent any strong movement toward excesses like those of the Continental inquisitorial system. If a jury was to have the power to determine guilt or innocence of the accused, the proceedings would necessarily have to be oral and

be conducted in the presence of the jury. Although it became the rule early in the development of the English criminal trial that the accuser need not employ and compensate the prosecuting attorney, the public prosecutor came very late to the common law. Even today, in England, a member of the practicing bar will be retained to represent the public interest in a criminal proceeding, and will be compensated from public funds. The development of a professional police force and of a public prosecutor, to investigate the commission of crimes, compile evidence, seek authority to prosecute, and actually conduct the criminal proceeding on behalf of the state, are comparatively recent developments in the common law world. In effect, they represent a shift away from the accusatorial and toward the inquisitorial system. But the public nature of the trial, the orality of the proceedings in the trial, the existence of a jury, and the limitations on the power of the judge, all combine to perpetuate some of the more desirable features of the accusatory system. The result is a kind of mixed system of criminal procedure.

In the civil law world, the movement toward the extremes of the inquisitorial model was impelled by the revival of Roman law, the influence of canonic procedure, and, most important, the rise of statism. The criminal action was an action by the state against the accused individual. The proceedings were written and secret. The accused had no right to counsel. He could be required to testify under oath, and torture was a common device for compelling testimony and eliciting proof. The judge was not limited to the role of impartial arbiter, but played an active part in the proceedings and determined their scope and nature. The prince, as the personification of the state, had the power to punish and to pardon, unrestricted by rules against ex post facto laws, by principles of equal treatment of individuals, or by what we would now call considerations of ordinary humanity and justice.

As a result of the work of Beccaria and others in the eighteenth century, public sentiment against the abuses of criminal procedure became very strong, and reform of criminal procedure became one of the principal objectives of the European revolutions. Reformers of the time pointed to the criminal procedure of England as an example of a just, democratic system, and called for reform of their own criminal

procedure along common law lines. Prominent among the demands made were (1) institution of the jury, (2) substitution of the oral public procedure in place of secret written procedure, (3) the establishment of the accused's right to counsel, (4) restriction of the judge's inquisitorial powers, (5) abolition of the requirement that the accused testify under oath, and (6) abolition of arbitrary intervention by the sovereign in the criminal process, by way of either penalty or pardon.

In the fervor of the French Revolution an attempt was made to abolish the criminal procedure of the old regime and substitute an entirely new one based on the English model. The failure of the effort to substitute a foreign tradition for an indigenous one soon became apparent, and a counterrevolution in criminal procedure took place in France. The result is a mixed system, composed in part of elements from prerevolutionary times and in part of reforms imposed after the Revolution.

The typical criminal proceeding in the civil law world can be thought of as divided into three basic parts: the investigative phase, the examining phase, and the trial. The investigative phase comes under the direction of the public prosecutor, who also participates actively in the examining phase, which is supervised by the examining judge. The examining phase is primarily written and is not public. The examining judge controls the nature and scope of this phase of the proceeding. He is expected to investigate the matter thoroughly and to prepare a complete written record, so that by the time the examining stage is complete, all the relevant evidence is in the record. If the examining judge concludes that a crime was committed and that the accused is the perpetrator, the case then goes to trial. If he decides that no crime was committed or that the crime was not committed by the accused, the matter does not go to trial.

In a very general way it can be said that the principal progress toward a more just and humane criminal proceeding in Europe in the last century and a half has come through reforms in the investigative and examining phases of the criminal proceeding. These reforms have been of two principal kinds. First, every effort has been made to develop a core of prosecuting attorneys who act impartially and objec-

tively. In Italy, for example, prosecuting attorneys are now members of the judiciary, having a security of tenure and consequent freedom from influence similar to that enjoyed by judges. Second, a number of procedural safeguards have been developed to assist the accused in protecting his own interests during the examining phase. Principal among these is the right of the accused to representation by counsel throughout this phase of the proceeding. This does not mean that counsel for the accused has unrestricted freedom to cross-examine witnesses or to introduce evidence on behalf of his client. The examining phase is still conducted by a judge. Counsel for the accused can, however, participate in the proceedings in such a way as to protect his client's interests, calling certain matters to the attention of the court and advising his client on how he should respond as the proceeding unfolds.

As a consequence of the nature of the examining phase of the criminal proceeding, the trial itself is different in character from the common law trial. The evidence has already been taken and the record made, and this record is available to the accused and his counsel, as well as to the prosecution. The function of the trial is to present the case to the trial judge and jury, and to allow the prosecutor and the defendant's counsel to argue their cases. It is also, of course, a public event, which by its very publicity tends to limit the possibility of arbitrary governmental action.

One frequently encounters two common misapprehensions about criminal procedure in the civil law world. One is to the effect that there is no presumption of innocence; the other is that there is no right to a jury trial. As stated, these are demonstrably false. Although the precise nature of the presumption and the degree to which it serves to protect the accused vary within the civil law world, it can be said that a legal presumption of innocence does exist in many civil law jurisdictions. In those in which it does not exist as a formal rule of law, something very much like it emerges from the examining phase of the criminal proceeding, where the character of the examining judge and judicialization of the function of the prosecuting attorney tend to prevent the trial of persons who are not probably guilty. The common supposition that there is no right to a jury trial in the civil

law world is simply contrary to the facts. The jury or its functional equivalent is an established institution since the reforms of the revolutionary period. It may not be available for as wide a range of offenses (even in some American states a jury trial is not granted in misdemeanor cases), it may not consist of twelve persons, it may frequently take the form of lay advisers who sit on the bench with the judge, and even where it looks like ours, it may not have to render a unanimous verdict of guilty in order for the accused to be convicted. These are, particularly when they accumulate, important differences between our conception of a jury and theirs. But the fact remains that the jury is a well established institution in the criminal proceedings of civil law jurisdictions.

For those who are concerned about the relative justice of the two systems, a statement made by an eminent scholar after long and careful study is instructive: he said that if he were innocent, he would prefer to be tried by a civil law court, but that if he were guilty, he would prefer to be tried by a common law court. This is, in effect, a judgment that criminal proceedings in the civil law world are more likely to distinguish accurately between the guilty and the innocent.

# XVIII

# PUBLIC LAW

CONSTITUTIONAL LAW and administrative law make up the basic content of what is called public law in civil law jurisdictions. Constitutional law is the law governing the organization and operation of the state. Administrative law is the law governing the organization and operation of the administrative branch of government and the relations of the administration with the legislature, the judiciary, and the public.

Earlier in this book, particularly in Chapters III and IV, we discussed the nature of the typical centralized state that emerged in Europe in the fifteenth to eighteenth centuries and blossomed in the Western revolutions. This was the modern nation-state—secular, positivist, internally and externally sovereign, a state whose power was exercised through the legislative, executive, and judicial branches of government. Among these, the representative legislature was the supreme power; legislation controlled executive and judicial action. Both legislative and executive action were immune from judicial review or interference.

Much of the development of public law in the civil law world since the revolutionary period can be viewed as a movement away from the extremes of this model. There are many fascinating, interrelated aspects to this movement, of which only two will be discussed here: the trend toward rigid constitutions and review of the constitutionality of legislation on the one hand, and the development of processes for reviewing the legality of administrative action (and hence curbing excessive administrative power) on the other.

In Chapter XIII we briefly discussed how the demand for review of the legality of administrative action was met. The widespread distrust of the judiciary, the traditional image of the judge and the judicial function, and the principle of separation of powers made such review by the ordinary judiciary an unacceptable solution. In addition,

the insistence that ordinary judges not be lawmakers in any sense led to rejection of the idea that prior judicial decisions should control future judicial action, even with respect to the same administrative act. The absence of such a principle would make judicial review of the legality of administrative action relatively ineffective. A court that was not bound by its own or other courts' prior decisions, and that consequently could make a decision binding only on the parties to the case before it, was inadequate to the task of keeping administrative action within acceptable bounds. What was needed was an acceptable method of deciding *erga omnes*—in a way that would have general effects, not limited to the parties—on the legality of the administrative act in question.

To give such powers to the ordinary courts would thus have required abandonment of a number of basic, deeply felt notions about the proper organization and operation of the state and about the nature and functions of the ordinary courts. As we have already seen, the solution adopted in France, and subsequently in much of the civil law world, was to establish a separate tribunal within the administration. In other nations, including Germany, the same result was achieved by setting up a separate system of administrative courts. Although there are many important differences between the two approaches typified by the French and German solutions, both met the same basic requirements. First, review of the legality of administrative action was kept out of the hands of the ordinary judiciary, and the principle of separation of powers was preserved. Second, a decision that an administrative act was illegal, and therefore void, could be given *erga omnes* effect without introducing the princple of *stare decisis* into the system of justice administered by the ordinary courts. Although there is great variety in the ways in which individual nations following the civil law tradition have worked out their systems for reviewing administrative legality, the basic pattern described here is the dominant one.

When one moves to the problem of reviewing the constitutionality of legislation, however, matters become more complicated. The difficulties perceived as standing in the way of an effective system of control are generally similar throughout the civil law world, but the move-

ment toward their definitive resolution is not nearly as advanced as that for review of the legality of administrative action. There clearly is a movement toward limiting legislative supremacy, but the pace of this movement and the range of solutions adopted vary from one civil law nation to another.

Legislative supremacy and a flexible constitution are companion concepts. If the expressed will of the representative legislature is to have the force of law, and if the legislative act is not subject to judicial or executive control, then it is an easy logical step to the conclusion that an ordinary law can prevail over a conflicting constitutional provision. This does not mean that the constitution loses all force as a basic law establishing a governmental structure and providing rules controlling and limiting governmental acts. Proposed legislation in a nation with a flexible constitution will still ordinarily be adopted within the limits established by current constitutional interpretation, and a proposal to transcend those limits will raise special legislative policy considerations. Where a possible conflict between a constitutional provision and a statute appears to have occurred without conscious legislative consideration, the tendency of the courts will be to interpret the provision and the statute in such a way as to avoid the conflict. In these and other ways, even a flexible constitution has it own special, *constitutional* character.

A flexible constitution, not surprisingly, is quite different from a rigid constitution. Here, however, it is necessary to distinguish between a formally rigid constitution and a functionally rigid one. Formally rigid constitutions, of which there are a number in the civil law world, specify limitations on legislative power and state special requirements for constitutional amendments, but they make no provision for enforcing these rules. The ordinary courts are, according to the prevailing theory, totally disqualified from interfering in the legislative process. The administrative courts can rule on the validity only of administrative acts, not of legislative acts. In form the legislature is bound by the constitution, but there is no organ of government authorized to decide whether the legislature has exceeded its powers. In a functionally rigid system, such an organ exists and functions.

The original, and still archetypal, example of a functionally rigid

constitutional system is that of the United States. The constitutional systems that appeared throughout the civil law world in the eighteenth and nineteenth centuries were sometimes rigid and sometimes flexible. None, however, included functional schemes for reviewing the constitutionality of legislation. The history of constitutional development in the civil law tradition since the revolution has been one of gradual movement toward functionally rigid constitutional systems. For a variety of reasons, however, the methods of reviewing the constitutional validity of legislative action adopted in civil law nations have been quite different from those used in the United States.

The movement toward constitutionalism in the civil law tradition can be seen as a logical reaction against the extremes of a secular, positivistic view of the state. During the period of the jus commune and prior to the Reformation, the authority of the Church and the writings of Roman Catholic natural lawyers about government and the individual provided a set of ideas and values that exerted some degree of restraining influence on the prince and on government officials. Many of these ideas were embedded deeply in the jus commune itself. But with the Reformation, the authority of the Church and of Roman Catholic natural law declined. With the growth of the nation-state the jus commune became a subsidiary system, inferior to the national law. At the same time the emphasis in secular natural law thinking on a popularly elected, representative legislature and on the separation of powers, combined with the revolutionary desire to limit the power of judges, produced an exaggerated emphasis on legislative autonomy. The old restraints on government were removed, and in the new positivistic state the representative legislature was given an inflated role and encouraged to be the sole judge of the legality (as opposed to the political acceptability) of its own action. In a sense the trend toward functionally rigid constitutions, with guarantees of individual rights against "unjust" legislative action, can be seen as a process of "codification of natural law" to fill the void left by rejection of Roman Catholic natural law and the jus commune on the one hand, and to deflate the bloated image of the legislature that emerged from the revolutionary period on the other.

A desire to review the constitutionality of legislative action does not

necessarily lead to the institution of *judicial* review. On the contrary, fundamental notions about the separation of powers and about the nature and limits of the judicial function in the civil law tradition make constitutional review by the ordinary judiciary an unacceptable alternative. And the rejection of the principle of *stare decisis* further limits the attractiveness of (ordinary) judicial review. Constitutional questions are of such far-reaching importance that it seems necessary to have them decided authoritatively, with *erga omnes* effects, rather than accept the hazards of inconsistent decisions by different courts, or even by the same court, in similar cases. But civil law nations cannot accept the proposal that the decisions of ordinary courts be given authority as law. Consequently the system familiar to citizens of the United States, in which all courts at every level of jurisdiction have the power to decide constitutional issues with *erga omnes* effects, has generally been rejected in the civil law world. Even where, as in some Latin American nations, some power of judicial review has been given to ordinary courts, the tendency has been to concentrate that power in one supreme court rather than diffuse it throughout the judicial system. This does not eliminate the possibility of conflicting decisions on the constitutionality of legislation, but it does reduce it. The Supreme Court of Chile, for example, is the only Chilean court with power to review the constitutionality of Chilean legislation. That court can decide similar cases differently, since Chile rejects *stare decisis*, but it is not likely to do so unless it is convinced that there are grave reasons for overruling its earlier decisions.

The ways in which demands for constitutional review of legislation have been gradually accommodated within the civil law tradition vary widely, although a trend toward the establishment of some form of constitutional review is evident. It is not surprising to find that France, the traditional source of the fundamentalist position on the separation of powers and the role of courts, has a system of nonjudicial review. The government organ that performs this function is called the Constitutional Council. This body is composed of all former Presidents of France plus nine additional persons, three of whom are chosen by the President of France, three by the President of the Chamber of Deputies, and three by the President of the Senate. Before promulga-

tion, certain kinds of laws must, and others may, be referred by the executive or the legislature to this council for a decision on their constitutionality. The council must respond within a certain time, after secret deliberations with no contentious procedure, no parties, no oral hearings, and no other marks of judicial proceedings. If the council finds the law in question unconstitutional, the law cannot be promulgated unless the Constitution is appropriately amended. The composition and procedure of the council make its nonjudicial nature clear. Its function seems more like an additional step in the legislative process than a judicial proceeding, and it is common to characterize this sort of constitutional review as political rather than judicial.

The stronger trend in the civil law world today, however, is toward the institution of some form of judicial review. We can best begin to understand this trend by examining another important distinction in constitutional doctrine: that between the formal and the substantive validity of legislation. The question of formal validity goes to whether the legislator has observed the rules set out in the statutes and the constitution to govern the form and procedure of the legislative process—such rules as those governing legislative deliberation, voting, and promulgation. Questions of substantive validity go to the consistency of the substance of the statute with constitutional provisions protecting the rights of the public and of government officials and agencies. (It might be noted that this distinction between formal and substantive validity, although conceptually clear, is difficult to maintain in practice. But that is a topic for another book.)

It is arguable that a formally defective statute is not really a statute, and that it therefore does not qualify as a part of "the law" that judges have the obligation to apply in cases before them. If the legislature has not followed the procedural rules established for the legislative process, according to this reasoning, the product is not legislation, and therefore need not be applied by the court. Even in a jurisdiction with a flexible constitution, according to this kind of thinking, the legislature must observe the formal rules in force in order to enact valid statutes. If it wishes to change the rules governing the formal lawmaking process, it must do so directly, by a statute enacted for that purpose, rather than by implication. At the same time the more funda-

mentalist view can be taken that even examination of the formal validity of legislation exceeds the judicial power and violates the principle of separation of powers. In revolutionary France this position had substantial support, but the tendency toward giving ordinary courts the power to review the formal validity of legislation has grown stronger. The generally prevailing doctrine has arrived at this position, although it still recognizes the power of the legislature to amend the *substantive* provisions of a flexible constitution simply by enacting legislation inconsistent with it.

In the case of a rigid constitution, however, conflicting legislation is by definition incapable of amending constitutional provisions. A direct amending process, usually more cumbersome and difficult than the ordinary legislative process, is required. In the presence of such a constitution, a good case can be made for giving an ordinary court the power to review the substantive validity of legislation. A law that conflicts with a substantive constitutional provision, so the reasoning goes, is not really a valid law because it exceeds the legislature's power, and it should therefore not be applied by the court. This is the theoretical basis of judicial review of constitutionality in the United States, as established in the famous case of *Marbury* v. *Madison*; and it has also been adopted in a few civil law jurisdictions in Latin America.

The trend toward judicial review of the constitutionality of legislation in the civil law world has been strong, particularly in this century. In general it can be said that the experience with review by ordinary courts, even where concentrated in one supreme court, has not been encouraging. The tendency has been for the civil law judge to recoil from the responsibilities and opportunities of constitutional adjudication. The tradition is too strong, the orthodox view of the judicial function too deeply ingrained, the effects of traditional legal education and career training too limiting. Concentrated judicial review by the Supreme Court has existed in Chile for forty years, but only a few statutes have been found unconstitutional in that time, and those usually in cases of minor importance. Judges have had the power of constitutional review in Japan for two decades, but the Japanese supreme court has yet to find a statute enacted by the Japanese parliament unconstitutional. Examples could be multiplied. This sort of experience, in

addition to the traditional civil law distrust of ordinary judges, the force of the doctrine of separation of powers, and the desire to give decisions of unconstitutionality *erga omnes* effects, explains the decision in Austria, Germany, and Italy, among other civil law nations, to establish separate constitutional courts. The analogy with the nineteenth century decision to establish separate tribunals for judicial review of the legality of administrative acts is clear.

The German and Italian constitutional courts were established after World War II, and represent the modern trend toward constitutional review in the civil law world. Although there are important differences between them, they share a number of significant characteristics. Both are separate courts, distinct from all others in their respective jurisdictions. Both have the exclusive power to decide on the constitutionality of legislation. In both Germany and Italy a decision by the constitutional court that a statute is unconstitutional is binding not only on the parties to the case but on all participants in the legal process. In both, the character of the proceedings and the rules governing the selection and tenure of judges give the constitutional court a definitely judicial character, in contrast to the political nature of the French Constitutional Council.

Generally, the procedure is this: in an action before a civil, criminal, administrative, or other court a party can raise a constitutional objection to a statute affecting the case. At this point the action is suspended, and the constitutional question is referred to the constitutional court for decision. When that decision is published, the original proceeding is resumed and conducted in accordance with it. If the constitutional court finds the statute constitutional, it can be applied in the proceeding; if the court rules it unconstitutional, the statute becomes invalid and cannot be applied in that specific proceeding or in any other. This procedure exemplifies the so-called "incidental" attack on constitutionality, in which the constitutional question is raised within the context of a specific judicial case or controversy in which the statute is applicable, but in which the case or controversy is the basis of jurisdiction and the constitutional question incidental to its resolution.

The incidental procedure, which permits a constitutional attack

only within the context of a specific case or controversy, is the only one available in the system of constitutional review in the United States. In Germany and Italy (and in other civil law countries, including Austria), however, a "direct" attack is also possible. Certain designated official agencies of government (and, in Germany, even individuals) can bring an action before the constitutional court to test the validity of a statute, even though there is no concrete dispute involving its application. In this way the limitations inherent in the restriction to incidental review in the United States are transcended, and a hearing can be had on the abstract question of constitutionality. The availability of the direct review procedure greatly expands the potential scope of constitutional review beyond that available in the United States.

It is clear that by first creating separate administrative courts, and later by establishing special constitutional courts, a number of civil law nations have moved a long way toward the ideal of what civil lawyers call the *Rechtstaat*: a system of government in which the acts of agencies and officials of all kinds are subject to the principle of legality, and in which procedures are available to interested persons to test the legality of governmental action and to have an appropriate remedy when the act in question fails to pass the test. A good argument can be made that the system of reviewing the legality of administrative action in the civil law world is more efficient and effective than ours. The development of an effective system of constitutional review of legislation in civil law countries has come much later than the American system, and it is still too early to judge how it will actually work over time. But the necessary parts all seem to be there, and the possibility exists that the range of legal protection against unconstitutional legislation within the civil law world may eventually exceed that available to citizens of the United States.

# XIX

## PERSPECTIVES

IT REMAINS to put the discussion in previous chapters into perspective, in order to correct some of the distortions that may have been caused by the selectivity, the emphasis, and the simplification that have necessarily characterized the prior discussion. One way the reader can acquire perspective is by further reading, and for this purpose a brief bibliography of recommended readings appears at the end of this chapter. The books and articles there cited themselves refer to other publications to which the still unsatisfied reader can go. That is really the better way to go about perfecting one's understanding of the civil law tradition, and this concluding chapter is a less satisfactory substitute.

One possible source of misunderstanding grows out of the difficulty of keeping our precise objective in mind. I have not attempted to describe any existing civil law system. Rather, I have sought to describe certain powerful historical events and currents of thought that have deeply influenced the growth of contemporary civil law systems and that give form and meaning to the legal rules, institutions, and processes that make up those systems. The precise legal rules in force differ widely from one civil law system to another. The specific solutions for typically recurring social problems that they embody are sometimes similar, but often they are quite different—even opposed. There is no divorce in Italy, but there is in Switzerland. A transfer of land is ineffective until entered in the land register in Germany, but such a register does not even exist in Belgium. The practice of law is a divided profession in France, but not in Chile. The decisory oath still exists in Italy but has been abolished in Austria. The organization, composition, and jurisdiction of courts in Spain is distinguishable in many ways from that in the Netherlands. The Mexican *amparo* is not the same thing as the Brazilian *mandado de seguranca*, and both

are markedly different from the Italian system of constitutional review.

Examples could easily be multiplied. Indeed, at the level of concrete application of a specific rule to a specific case by a specific court in a specific proceeding, it would be hard to find two civil law systems that would operate in the same way to produce the same results. The resultant of the forces represented by the substantive rules, procedures, and institutions that come into play in the decision of a case in one nation is almost invariably different from the resultant of analogous forces in another. The emphasis has been not on the differences but on what these legal systems have in common, on what it is that relates them to each other in a way that makes it possible to contrast them with other legal families, the products of other legal traditions.

However, there is an analogous problem in talking about the civil law tradition itself. The impact of the various components of that tradition has varied from one nation to another. Consider German legal science; it has never taken deep root in France, but the Italians have, in this sense, become more German than the Germans. Consider the ideology of the French Revolution and the effect it had on the form, style, and content of the Code Napoléon; the German Civil Code represents a conscious rejection of a number (but not all) of the premises of the French codification. Civil codes enacted in this century show the influences of both. Consider the Roman civil law. It grew up in Italy, it was formally received in Germany, it was gradually absorbed in France, with different consequences for each system. The extent of influence of indigenous law is another variable. In Italy, the jus commune was indigenous law, but in some European nations separate local legal customs and institutions were consciously preserved, glorified, and integrated into the new unified legal order of the state. In others, such as Spain, regional indigenous legal characteristics have been retained as locally applicable law (the *fueros* of Catalonia, Aragon, and other formerly independent kingdoms).

The age of a code is another important variable. For example, the civil codes in force in civil law jurisdictions vary in age from the Code Napoléon of 1804, still in force in France, to shiny new postwar civil codes in some nations. The problems involved in interpreting and

applying very old codes are of course quite different from those encountered with very new ones. The old codes are products of a different time, and do not speak to a great range of contemporary problems that are the express concern of the new code. Two principal consequences flow from the failure to modernize the old codes: one is the tendency to impede economic and social change; the other, much more important, is the imposition of a greater burden on judicial interpretation as a progressive element in the legal process. The greater the gap between what society needs and what the code says, the greater the tendency for courts to develop new interpretations of old code provisions in order to meet the need. Judicial decisions become in fact, if not in theory, a source of law.

France, with the oldest civil code, is the prime example. Great areas of French law are judicial creations out of inadequate statutory materials. Even though formal respect is paid to the provisions of the code, the fiction that these provisions actually offer solutions to the problems that come before the courts has been worn thin by more than a century and a half of creative judicial lawmaking. All know that much of the law actually in force is found in the reports of judicial decisions, not in the Code Napoléon. In time such a tendency strongly affects the real distribution of power between legislature and judiciary, shifting that distribution away from the model of the legal process that emerged from the French Revolution.

The actual operation of the legal order within civil law nations is thus affected both by the age of the codes in force and by the judicial response to the adequacy of old codes. In France much of the power of the old code to impede social and economic progress has been reduced by a creative judiciary. But in some civil law nations, particularly those outside Europe, old codes of the French type are applied by a judiciary that still sees itself, and is still seen by others, in the image that emerged from the French Revolution. The result is a lack of judicial response to the needs of a changing society and economy. While embracing the French style of code and the French revolutionary image of the judge and the legislator, such nations have often failed to develop the pragmatic French solution of a covertly but effectively creative judiciary.

Consequently it is necessary to emphasize that the precise mixture

of local influences and of components of the civil law tradition, the precise timing of such important events as the enactment of the codes in force, and the precise extent of French-Italian and German influence on the legal process varies widely throughout the civil law world. This adds another series of variables to the differing substantive rules of law, legal institutions, and legal processes. Civil law nations share the civil law tradition, but they share it in different degrees.

Another possible source of distortion in this account of the civil law tradition is the necessarily selective nature of the discussion. We have examined only a few readily identifiable characteristics of this tradition, and although these are probably the most important, we should not forget that they are not the only ones. For example, we have not discussed in any detail the strength of the royal tradition in Europe or the survival, beyond the time of the French Revolution, of a number of institutions and attitudes whose origins are traceable primarily to the absolute monarchies. We have not lingered over the proposition, for which there is a good deal of historical evidence, that nations once subject to absolute rule have found it easy to slip back into absolutism in one form or another. We have not considered the fact that the executive branches of all European governments were originally creations of the monarchies, and we have avoided discussing the importance of these origins in understanding the peculiar ways in which legal controls over administrative actions have evolved in the civil law tradition. We have not commented on the growing professionalization of government administration, or on the tendency for it to become a distinctive career, often (particularly in Germany) dominated by lawyers. Many other examples could be cited, for we have only touched the surface in this book.

The legal tradition is a part of the culture, a very old, deeply rooted, firmly held part. The relations between basic legal ideas and similarly profound social, economic, and political attitudes is extremely close and extremely complex. The law both draws meaning from and supplies meaning to the rest of the culture, and is inseparable from it. We have tried to understand some of these interrelationships, but it would be a mistake to assume that we have exhausted the subject.

From time to time certain aspects of the civil law tradition have

been criticized expressly or by implication. In particular, it has been suggested that there is something excessive about the emphasis on a sharp separation of powers; that the effort to make the law judge-proof is both futile and, in the long run, socially undesirable; that the quest for certainty has become both a romantic form of snark-hunting and a meaningless, catchword argument, available to support any position; that the role of the legislature has become bloated out of all proportion, far beyond the ability of that institution to meet the demands placed upon it; that the premises and methods of German legal science have isolated the law from the problems of the society it is supposed to serve, while perpetuating a set of socioeconomic assumptions that are no longer valid, if they ever were; that the civil law is dominated by a misdirected scholarly tradition, diverting the great potential influence and the enormous energy, creativity, and cultivated intelligence of civil law teacher-scholars into essentially arid pursuits.

These are not merely the reactions of an American lawyer to the prominently exotic features of an inadequately understood foreign legal tradition. Such criticisms are not original with common lawyers. They are all made by civil lawyers themselves, critically examining their own law and calling for its reform. This brings us to a third possible source of misunderstanding: the assumption that the civil law tradition today is both monolithic and static. It is neither.

What I have described as the civil law tradition is, first of all, a set of dominant influences and attitudes, those that stand out among a variety of competing historical and intellectual forces, the ones that have emerged most prominently from the competition for acceptance. The model of the positivistic state that emerged from the thought of the seventeenth and eighteenth centuries and from the revolution represented a victory for its adherents over the strongly held views of natural law proponents and the advocates of other forms of social and political organization. The Roman civil law–jus commune competed with native legal traditions for dominance of the unified national legislation of France and Germany. German legal science was only one set of attitudes about the objectives and methods of legal scholarship and the nature and functions of the legal order. At every point in the history of the civil law tradition a variety of forces have been at work.

This is particularly true today. Every aspect of the law is under critical examination by legal scholars, who question not only specific rules, institutions, and processes, but also the basic components of the legal tradition that give the positive legal order form and meaning. The orthodoxy of the time is constantly under attack. We have seen only the most prominent and durable components of a pluralistic legal tradition.

Just as the civil law tradition is far from monolithic, so is it in constant transition. The dominant characteristics described in this book represent only one stage in a process that began nearly twenty-five centuries ago and can be expected to continue long into the future. The Roman civil law alone has passed through many phases—preclassical and classical law, Justinian's *Corpus Juris Civilis*, the commentaries of the Glossators and the Commentators, the writings of the Humanists, the French codification, the theories of Savigny and the historical school, and the BGB. And this is only one strand in the fabric of the civil law tradition. The canon law began as a law of and for the Church, grew in spiritual jurisdiction as the Church's power spread, and eventually was extended when the ecclesiastical tribunals acquired temporal jurisdiction; it made an important contribution to the jus commune, and, after the Reformation, disappeared as a major continuing influence on the development of the civil law tradition. The commercial law began as a group of customary practices created by pragmatic merchants to meet their own needs. Eventually commercial law and commercial courts were nationalized, becoming a part of the official apparatus of the state, together with separate commercial codes. Today the separate commercial courts are disappearing, and there is a similar trend with respect to separate commercial codes.

Since the early nineteenth century there has been a gradually accelerating movement away from the extremes of the revolutionary model of the legal process. The extension of the power of statutory interpretation by the ordinary courts was an important early step, supported by the growing practice of publishing and citing judicial opinions. The creation of tribunals to review the legality of administrative action was another. Even where such tribunals were historically a part of the administration, as in France, they now look and act like courts. Despite

rejection of the doctrine of *stare decisis*, the practice of courts is to decide similar cases similarly, in much the same way as do common law courts. More recently the adoption of rigid constitutions, filling the gap left by the rejection of natural law as a check on the legislature, has been accompanied by a variety of devices to keep legislation within constitutional limits. There has been a substantial shift of power from legislature to court (and also from legislature to executive, but that is another topic), eroding the ideal of legislative supremacy. The powers of courts both to review the legality of administrative action and the constitutionality of legislative action, and to interpret statutes, undermine the dogma of strict separation of powers. A legal process designed to make the law judge-proof has become steadily more judicialized, and today the rate of judicialization is accelerating throughout the civil law world.

German legal science has been the object of satire, ridicule, and direct attack by legal thinkers in Germany and elsewhere from the time of its emergence. More recently, and particularly since World War II, its critics have begun to have more effect. There is a growing group of scholars who call for a fresh approach to legal scholarship. Some of them demand rejection of all that legal science has accomplished. Others treat legal science as a valid but spent phase in the evolution of the civil law tradition; they wish to preserve the gains made by it, particularly the provision of order and system in the law, and build on them. All agree that the purity of legal science—its rejection of everything considered nonlegal—has had the effect of separating law from the life of the society whose problems should be its basic concern. This social, economic, and political agnosticism has cut the law off from the rest of the culture, and made lawyers less and less relevant to social needs. At the same time, the social and economic assumptions that are embodied in the abstract conceptions of legal science seem to some critics to conflict with the contents of modern constitutions and the programs of modern governments. The argument is made that emphasis on the private legal relation, the subjective right, and the private juridical act (described in Chapter XI) perpetuates an individualistic, nineteenth century form of economic and social Darwinism, impeding governmental redistribution of power, status,

and wealth, and makes the law and lawyers, often unconsciously, into reactionary forces. Such criticisms have special force and relevance in developing nations within the civil law world, particularly in Latin America. There the argument can be most persuasively made that the legal process is lagging behind the rest of the culture, sometimes inadequate as a vehicle for economic and social change that should be put into legal form, sometimes inherently opposed to such change, and with increasing frequency irrelevant to it.

These kinds of dissatisfaction with legal science have been reinforced by a shift in the legal order's center of gravity. The bastion of legal science has traditionally been private law, and particularly Roman civil law. Until recently, the civil code has served something like a constitutional function in civil law systems, providing a scheme of private rights which it was the primary business of government to protect and enforce. General principles and general theories of law, derived primarily from the materials of private law, dominated the legislative and judicial processes. As a result, the civil code and the doctrinal work of civil lawyers furnished the ideological fuel of the legal process. But with the adoption of modern rigid constitutions embodying new social and economic conceptions, and with the establishment of judicial review of the constitutionality of legislation in important civil law nations, the legal center of gravity has begun to undergo what promises to be a drastic shift from civil code to constitution, from private law to public law, from ordinary court to constitutional court, from legislative positivism to constitutional principle. The provisions of such constitutions are an alternative source of general principles; they offer an alternative set of notions to guide judges in the interpretation and application of statutes, including the provisions of civil codes. The power of constitutional or other courts to find statutes invalid *erga omnes* lends great authority to constitutional provisions. In legal systems where a modern rigid constitution coupled with judicial review confronts a strong tradition of legal science, as is the case in Germany and Italy today, a fundamental readjustment of the legal process is under way. It is too early to predict with any confidence what the ultimate result will be, but it seems certain that the role of legal science within the civil law tradition is shrinking.

With these perspectives on the variety, complexity, and dynamism of the civil law tradition in mind, we turn at last to a brief consideration of the most fascinating perspective of all: the comparative. If the reader is like most amateurs of comparative law, he has looked impatiently through this book for the answers to two great questions. What is the difference between the common law and the civil law? Which is better? Each of these questions provides an appropriate topic for another book. Neither can be answered here, but a few comments on each are in order.

First, what is the difference? A good deal of this sort of comparison has been stated or implied, often on the assumption that the reader has a general familiarity with his own legal tradition, throughout this discussion. The reader has already acquired some notions about fundamental differences between the two legal traditions. But unless he has an unusually thorough and sophisticated knowledge of the common law, he is ill-equipped for thorough comparative consideration even of those matters that were selected for discussion in this book. And it is hardly necessary to add that any sort of adequate comparison would require the consideration of a multitude of topics that we have not discussed at all. This book does not answer the question "What is the difference?" It merely indicates what some of the differences are and describes something of their origins and their significance.

Which is better? At one level this is a foolish question. It is like asking whether the French language is superior to the English language. Better for whom? Surely no one would suggest that the Italians would be better off with the common law tradition, or the Americans with the civil law. The law is rooted in the culture, and it responds, within cultural limits, to the specific demands of a given society in a given time and place. It is, at bottom, a historically determined process by which certain social problems are perceived, formulated, and resolved. Substitution of one legal tradition for another is neither possible nor desirable.

At a different level the question becomes more respectable: to what extent does the legal tradition respond to the demands legitimately made on it by a given society? To what extent does the tradition impede the realization of worthy political, economic, and social objec-

tives? Are civil law nations more adequately served by their legal systems than are common law nations? A moment's reflection on such questions produces others. By what critera can we make this kind of judgment? How does one evaluate degrees of satisfaction of complex social, economic, and political demands? How can one even determine clearly what such demands are? There may be satisfactory ways of answering these questions, but it is obvious that they extend far beyond the range of this book.

We can, however, recognize the subtlety and complexity of the differences between the two legal traditions, and come to understand how a misunderstanding of those differences can affect all forms and phases of international dealings. The easy judgments, the thoughtless assumptions that people within both traditions commonly make about foreign legal systems are a constant source of misunderstanding and justified irritation. They get in the way of international negotiations. They cripple foreign aid programs. They limit the effectiveness of cultural exchange. They misdirect effort and misallocate resources. A person who would not think of going to a foreign nation without some understanding of its history, politics, language, and literature will almost invariably arrive in total ignorance of one of the oldest and most important elements of its culture: its legal tradition.

It is unlikely, although it might be desirable, that thoughtful comparative lawyers will regularly be included in the teams that formulate foreign policies and programs at various governmental and private levels within the common law world. It is only slightly less unlikely that they will regularly be called upon to participate in the elaboration and execution of such policies and programs. One reason is that there are too few of them, although that problem might be remedied if the demand existed. But the main reason is that the demand is not there. Comparative lawyers have failed to sensitize others, lawyers and non-lawyers alike, to the realization that something important is missing from the array of expertise customarily brought to bear on relations with nations in the civil law world.

What is missing is the realization that there is something out there in the civil law world that is important and different. It is more than a set of different legal rules. It is not summed up in stereotypes about

civil law codes and common law judicial decisions. It is subtler than that, and more pervasive. It has historical, political, social—in a word, cultural—dimensions. Anyone, lawyer or nonlawyer, who wants to understand Western Europe and Latin America (or, for that matter, the civil law nations of the Middle East, Asia, and Africa) must become familiar with the civil law tradition.

RECOMMENDED READINGS

# RECOMMENDED READINGS

## On the Civil Law Generally

René David and John E. C. Brierly. *Major Legal Systems in the World Today*. London: Stevens & Sons, 1968.

This work, basically a translation of David's important book *Les Grandes Systèmes de droit contemporains*, contains a discussion (pp. 21–118) of what he calls "The Romano-Germanic Family." Professor David talks about a number of matters that I have discussed, but his emphasis and point of view are often quite different.

K. W. Ryan. *An Introduction to the Civil Law*. Brisbane: The Law Book Company of Australasia, 1962.

This is a useful survey of the principal rules and institutions of the civil law, but it is based almost entirely on French and German law. The book includes an excellent but overly brief historical and general descriptive introduction.

Rudolph B. Schlesinger. *Comparative Law: Cases-Text-Materials*. 2d ed. Brooklyn: Foundation Press, 1959.

Arthur Taylor Von Mehren. *The Civil Law System: Cases and Materials for the Comparative Study of Law*. Boston: Little, Brown, 1957.

Schlesinger and Von Mehren have prepared their books for use in law school courses, and the material is likely to baffle those who are unaccustomed to law school textbooks. Schlesinger's is the easier of the two and therefore the more useful for the general reader. Both books contain much material of interest and many bibliographical references. In particular, see Schlesinger's "Dialogue," pp. 201–48, and his bibliography, pp. 499–600.

## On Elements of the Civil Law Tradition

### Roman Law

F. H. Lawson. *A Common Lawyer Looks at the Civil Law*. Ann Arbor: University of Michigan Law School, 1953.

This delightful book consists of a set of lectures whose principal topic is the influence of Roman law on contemporary civil law. In addition, the author illuminates many other aspects of the civil law tradition with style, wit, and insight. Essential reading.

Hans Julius Wolff. *Roman Law: An Historical Introduction*. Norman: University of Oklahoma Press, 1951.

An excellent historical survey. The last chapter, describing the evolution of Roman civil law after Justinian's compilation, is particularly recommended.

## Canon Law

*A General Survey of Events, Sources, Persons, and Movements in Continental Legal History*. Boston: Little, Brown, 1912.

Part IX is a 20-page discussion of canon law in European legal history.

John Henry Wigmore. *A Panorama of the World's Legal Systems*. Washington, D.C.: Washington Law Book Company, 1928.

Chapter XIV of this illustrated survey is devoted to canon law.

## Commercial Law

W. A. Bewes. *The Romance of the Law Merchant*. London: Sweet and Maxwell, 1923.

William Mitchell. *An Essay on the Early History of the Law Merchant*. Cambridge, Eng.: Cambridge University Press, 1904.

Mitchell's is the better book and more demanding of the reader. Bewes's work is simpler and somewhat erratically romantic. Both are quite brief.

## The Role of Judges

John P. Dawson. *The Oracles of the Law*. Ann Arbor: University of Michigan Law School, 1968.

This book describes, in rich detail, the development of the judicial traditions in Rome, England, France, and Germany from early times to the twentieth century. Although the prose style is eminently readable, this book may provide heavy going for the amateur of comparative law; but it is worth the effort.

## On the Law of Specific Nations or Areas

### France

René David and Henry P. De Vries. *The French Legal System: An Introduction to Civil Law Systems*. Dobbs Ferry, N.Y.: Oceana Publications, 1958.

This excellent short book surveys the French legal system in a readable and authoritative style.

F. H. Lawson, E. A. Anton, and L. Neville Brown, eds. *Amos & Walton's Introduction to French Law*. 2d ed. Oxford: Clarendon Press, 1963.

This work is more recent and more substantial than that by David and De Vries. If one had to choose between them, one might quite reasonably read *Amos & Walton*, but it is better to read both.

## Germany

E. J. Cohn. *Manual of German Law*. Vol. I. Dobbs Ferry, N.Y.: Oceana Publications, 1968.

Chapters 1 and 2 of this excellent work provide brief introductions to the German legal system and to the general part of the civil law.

Gesellschaft für Rechtsvergleichung. *Bibliographie des deutschen Rechts*. Karlsruhe: Verlag C. F. Müller, 1964.

The first part of this book contains a valuable brief description, in English, of the principal features of the German legal system.

## Italy

Mauro Cappelletti, John Henry Merryman, and Joseph M. Perillo. *The Italian Legal System: An Introduction*. Stanford, Calif.: Stanford University Press, 1967.

This is the only book in English on the contemporary legal system of Italy.

## Latin America

Helen Clagett. *The Administration of Justice in Latin America*. Dobbs Ferry, N.Y., 1952.

A short but useful survey of Latin American judicial systems.

Kenneth L. Karst. *Latin American Legal Institutions: Problems for Comparative Study*. Los Angeles: UCLA Latin American Center, 1966.

Although intended for use in law school courses, this book contains a wealth of fascinating material and is so well organized that it is highly accessible to nonlawyers.

On the law of specific Latin American countries, see the series, published by the Law Library of the U.S. Library of Congress, of works by various authors titled "The Law and Legal Literature of—." The nations included in the series are Argentina, Bolivia, Brazil, Chile, Colombia, Ecuador, Mexico, Paraguay, Peru, Uruguay, and Venezuela. Although these works have a heavy bibliographical bias, they also include a good deal of descriptive information about the legal systems.

# INDEX

# INDEX

169